José Me...
Ex-profesor de ...
Instituto Británico y de la Escuela ...
&
Anglo-Didáctica Linguistics Group

Grammar
&
Humour

Aprenda inglés con una sonrisa
Learn English with a Smile

Second Edition
(Revised)

ANGLO DIDACTICA
PUBLISHING

2ª edición.
© José Merino Bustamante
© Editorial Anglo Didáctica, S.L.
Diseño de cubierta: Equipo de diseño de la editorial.
The image and cliparts used on the cover of this book are from:
Art Explosion 600,000 Nova Development CD-ROM, Corel Gallery Magic 200,000 CD-Rom and Corel Gallery FunArt CD-Rom

No unauthorized photocopying

Todos los derechos reservados. Ninguna parte de esta publicación, incluido el diseño de la cubierta, puede ser reproducida, almacenada o transmitida de ninguna forma, ni por ningún medio, sea éste electrónico, químico, mecánico, electro-óptico, grabación, fotocopia o cualquier otro, sin la previa autorización escrita por parte de la Editorial.

Impreso en España.
Printed in Spain.
ISBN: 84-86623-95-2
Depósito legal: M-4659-2002.

Anglo Didáctica Publishing
C/ Santiago de Compostela, 16
28034 Madrid – Spain.
Tel y fax: (34) 91 378 01 88.

Impreso por Fareso, S.A.
Paseo de la Dirección, 5 – 28039 Madrid.

ÍNDICE

		Páginas
	Presentación	1
I	Verbos *to be* y *to have* en presente y pasado	3
II	Presente habitual *(Simple present)*. Uso del auxiliar *do*. Presente continuo *(Continuous present)*	6
III	Imperativo *(Imperative)*	18
IV	Pretérito indefinido *(Simple past)*. Uso del auxiliar *did*. Pretérito imperfecto *(Past continuous)*. Verbos regulares e irregulares	21
V	Pretérito perfecto *(Present perfect)*. Verbos regulares e irregulares	36
VI	Pluscuamperfecto *(Pluperfect)*	47
VII	Futuro *(Future)*	48
VIII	Verbos defectivos o anómalos *(Defective or anomalous verbs)*	55
IX	Pronombres relativos *(Relative pronouns)*	80
X	Oraciones condicionales *(Conditional sentences)*	92
XI	Gerundio *(Gerund)*	98
XII	Voz pasiva *(Passive voice)*	108
	Ejercicios	114
	Soluciones	121
	Puntos lingüísticos	125
	Frases hechas	129
	Vocabulario	131

PRESENTACION

En este libro, que esperamos resulte divertido a la vez que útil, se recoge una antología del humor británico, especialmente adaptada para estudiantes de inglés.

Para formar esta selección se han escogido chistes que se prestan a un estudio gramatical.

Se ha estructurado la obra de acuerdo con un criterio de progresión. Se comienza con chistes que contienen principalmente los verbos *to be* y *to have,* para seguir con otros de estructuras más complicadas, como el presente habitual, el continuo, los pasados, etc.

Cada chiste va acompañado de notas aclaratorias y comentarios gramaticales o explicaciones sobre los juegos de palabras que fundamentan la comicidad de muchas de las historias.

Sigue a la selección de chistes una serie de ejercicios, con soluciones, basados en las estructuras gramaticales estudiadas.

Asimismo se incluyen sendas relaciones en las que se recogen puntos de interés lingüístico y frases hechas que aparecen en el libro, las cuales pueden utilizarse en diversos contextos.

Por último se ha introducido un vocabulario bilingüe de aquellas palabras que puedan ofrecer dificultad para la comprensión de los textos.

J. M.

I VERBOS *TO BE* Y *TO HAVE* EN PRESENTE Y PASADO

1

BRIAN: «Girls are more beautiful than boys.»
KATE: «Naturally!»
BRIAN: «Naturally? Not naturally. Artificially!»

girls are more beautiful than boys, las chicas son más guapas que los chicos. Hay que notar el empleo de *than* en una oración comparativa.
are es una de las tres formas del presente de *to be*. Se emplea con las segundas personas (singular y plural) así como con la primera y tercera personas del plural.

2

Overheard at a wedding reception.
MAN: «Are you a friend of the bridegroom's?»
WOMAN: «No, I'm not. I'm the bride's mother.»

wedding reception, recepción que se da en una boda.
are you a friend of the bridegroom's?, ¿es usted una amiga del novio? Este es un caso del llamado, en inglés, *double genitive*, que es una combinación de *periphrastic* e *inflected genitives*.
I'm the bride's mother, soy la madre del novio. He aquí el caso más corriente del genitivo sajón, llamado *inflected genitive*, que consiste en colocar un apóstrofo y *s* al poseedor, seguido de lo que se posee. ‖ *I'm* es la contracción de *I am*. ‖ *bride* es «novia» y *bridegroom*, «novio» durante la ceremonia.

3

At a party.
MRS ARMSTRONG: «I'm Mr Armstrong's wife.»
BEAUTIFUL BLONDE: «I'm his secretary.»
MRS ARMSTRONG: «Oh, were you?»

I'm his secretary, yo soy su secretaria. Nótese el uso del adjetivo posesivo *his*, ya que se refiere a *Mr Amstrong*.
were you?, ¿era usted? || *were* es una de las dos formas del pasado de *to be*. Se emplea con las segundas personas (singular y plural) así como con la primera y tercera personas del plural.

4

KAY: «My uncle Ted had a wooden leg.»
PHIL: «That's nothing compared with my cousin Albert. He had a mahogany chest.»

my uncle Ted had a wooden leg, mi tío Ted tenía una pierna de madera. || *had* es el pasado de *to have* (tener).
that's nothing compared with my cousin Albert, eso no tiene comparación con mi primo A. o eso no se puede comparar con mi primo A. Literalmente: «eso es nada comparado con mi primo A.» || *that's* es la contracción de *that is,* «eso es». || *is* en la forma del verbo *to be* en presente, que se emplea con la tercera persona del singular. || *chest* puede ser «pecho» (tórax) y también «cómoda» (mueble), «cofre», de ahí el chiste.

5

At the chemist's.
ELDERLY LADY: «Have you anything for grey hair?»
SHOP-ASSISTANT: «I have nothing except all my respect, madam.»

at the chemist's, en la farmacia. Este es un caso del llamado *local genitive.*
have you anything for grey hair? ¿tiene usted algo para las canas? ‖ *have* es una de las dos formas del verbo *to have* en presente. Se emplea con las primeras y segundas personas (singular y plural) así como con la tercera personal del plural. ‖ *grey hair* = pelo gris.

II PRESENTE HABITUAL *(SIMPLE PRESENT)*.
USO DEL AUXILIAR *DO*.
PRESENTE CONTINUO *(CONTINUOUS PRESENT)*.

6

A tourist arrives at a village when the church bells are ringing and asks a villager:
—«Why are the bells ringing today?»
—«Because the priest is pulling the ropes», he answers.

a tourist arrives at a village, un turista llega a un pueblo. Hay que observar el uso de *at* después del verbo *arrive* al mencionar un lugar que no es un nombre propio. Compárese con *to arrive in Madrid*, llegar a Madrid; *to arrive in Spain*, llegar a España. ‖ Nótese la tercera persona del singular del presente del verbo *arrive*, con «s».

when the church bells are ringing, cuando las campanas de la iglesia están tocando. Se utiliza el presente continuo porque describe una acción larga que sucede en un momento determinado.

7

GEORGE: «What goes peck, bang; peck, bang; peck, bang?»
TOMMY: «I dont't know. I give up. What is it, George?»
GEORGE: «Three hens in a mine-field.»

what goes peck, bang? ¿qué hace «peck, bang»? De igual manera: *the dog goes wow*, el perro hace «guau».
I don't know, no lo sé. Nótese la omisión del equivalente al pronombre español *lo* en este caso.
I give up, me doy por vencido.

8

Angela is telling a story to Judy.
ANGELA: «There was a tap on the door...»
JUDY: «A tap on the door?»
ANGELA: «Yes.»
JUDY: «Funny sense of humour the plumber's got!»

Angela is telling a story to Judy, A. está contando una historia a J. Se usa el presente continuo porque ocurre en un momento dado.
there was a tap on the door, llamaron a la puerta. Literalmente: «hubo (o había) un golpecito en la puerta». ‖ *tap* también puede significar «grifo», de ahí el chiste.
funny sense of humour the plumber's got! ¡qué sentido del humor tiene el fontanero! ‖ *the plumber's got = the plumber has got*. El verbo *to have* seguido de *got* significa «tener». Otros ejemplos: *I've (I have) got five pounds*, tengo cinco libras; *he's (he has) got a dictionary*, él tiene un diccionario.

9

Gossiping.
LOUISE: «Betsy is getting married tomorrow.»
ROSE: «Who's the lucky man?»
ANDY: «Her father.»

gossiping, cotilleando, de cotilleo.
Betsy is getting married tomorrow, Isabelita se casa mañana. El presente continuo con un adverbio que indique futuro sirve también para describir una acción futura. ‖ *Betsy* es una variante de *Betty*.
who's the lucky man? ¿quién es el hombre afortunado? ‖ *who's* es la contracción de *who is*.
her father, su padre. Nótese el uso del adjetivo posesivo *her*, ya que se refiere a *Betsy*.

10

POLICEMAN: «Why are you driving so fast?»
WOMAN DRIVER: «Well, officer, the thing is that my brakes are out of order and I want to get home as soon as possible to avoid an accident.»

the thing is that my brakes are out of order, lo que sucede es que no me funcionan los frenos. Literalmente: «la cosa es que mis frenos están estropeados.»
I want to get home, quiero llegar a casa.
as soon as possible, cuanto antes.
to avoid an accident, para evitar un accidente.

11

MARION: «Is your aunt Peggy rich?»
FREDDY: «Rich! She has so many gold teeth that she sleeps with her head inside a safe.»

gold teeth, dientes de oro.
that she sleeps with her head inside a safe, que duerme con la cabeza dentro de una caja fuerte. Nótese el adjetivo *her* en este caso, que en español se traduce por el artículo determinado. ‖ El verbo *sleeps* lleva «s» porque se trata de la primera persona del singular del presente.

12

At a restaurant.
SARAH: «Why are you eating your chop so quickly?»
BARBARA: «Well, it has a strange taste, so I'm eating it quickly just to get rid of it.»

why are you eating your chop so quickly? ¿por qué te comes la chuleta tan deprisa? Se emplea el presente continuo porque describe una acción que sucede en el momento en que se habla.
it has a strange taste, tiene un gusto muy raro.
just to get rid of it, para terminar cuanto antes. Literalmente: «para librarme de ella». La palabra *just,* en este caso, sirve para dar énfasis a la idea.

13

MRS PARKER: «Do you manage all right on your husband's salary?»
MRS CARTER: «Yes, the only snag is that there's always too much month left at the end of the money.»

do you manage all right on your husband's salary? ¿te las arreglas bien con el sueldo de tu marido? Adviértase la preposición *on*. ‖ *do* se usa en oraciones interrogativas en presente con todas las personas menos con la tercera persona del singular.

there's always too much month left at the end of the money, siempre queda demasiado mes al final del dinero. ‖ La expresión *there's something left* significa «queda, sobra algo».

14

JAKE: «This car has wonderful brakes. No matter how fast you drive you always stop dead. Let's go for a ride and try them.»
KEN: «No, thank you. I prefer to stop alive.»

no matter how fast you drive, por muy deprisa que se conduzca. Literalmente: «no importa cuán deprisa conduzcas».
you always stop dead, siempre se para en seco. ‖ El chiste reside en la expresión *to stop dead,* parar en seco, literalmente «parar muerto» y la contestación: *I prefer to stop alive,* yo prefiero parar vivo. ‖ Nótese los opuestos: *dead / alive.*

15

At an examination.
INVIGILATOR (to examinee): «You look a bit puzzled. Have you any difficulty with the first question, Newman?»
EXAMINEE: «Oh no, I have no difficulty at all with any of the questions. I only have some trouble with the answers.»

you look a bit puzzled, pareces un poco perplejo. El verbo *look* seguido de un adjetivo significa «parecer».
I have no difficulty at all, no tengo ninguna dificultad. ‖ *at all,* precedido de negación, quiere decir «en absoluto» y sirve para dar énfasis a la idea.

16

In the English literature class. The teacher asks this question:
—«What was the name of Shakespeare's wife?»
No pupil seems to know the answer. Suddenly, Jim puts up his hand and says:
—«I know, sir: It was Mrs Shakespeare.»

the teacher asks this question, el profesor hace esta pregunta. ‖ *to ask a question*, hacer una pregunta.
no pupil seems to know the answer, ningún alumno parece saber la respuesta.
Jim puts up his hand, J. levanta la mano. Obsérvese que los verbos *asks*, *seems* y *puts* llevan «s» porque se trata de terceras personas del singular del presente.
El nombre de la esposa de Shakespeare era Anne Hathaway.

17

WILLY: «I don't like grapes.»
TERRY: «Why not?»
WILLY: «I like wine by itself, not in capsules.»

I like wine by itself, me gusta el vino por sí solo. Nótese la omisión del artículo delante de *wine* porque se trata de una generalización.

18

TELEPHONE OPERATOR: «It costs two pounds to speak to someone in Birmingham.»
MAN ON THE PHONE: «Isn't there a cheaper rate for just listening? I want to call my wife».

it costs two pounds to speak to someone in Birmingham, cuesta dos libras hablar con alguien en B. Nótese *to speak to* «hablar con».
isn't there a cheaper rate for just listening? ¿no hay una tarifa más barata para escuchar solamente? Hay que notar la forma *-ing* del verbo *listen* después de *for*.

19

At a shoe shop.
CUSTOMER: «I want a pair of crocodile shoes, please.»
SHOP-ASSISTANT: «Yes, sir. What size does your crocodile take?»

shoe shop, zapatería.
what size does your crocodile take? ¿qué número gasta su cocodrilo? ‖ *size* = tamaño; *take* = tomar. ‖ *does* se usa en preguntas con la tercera persona del singular del presente.

20

MR RICHARDS: «Doctor, I want to thank you for your wonderful treatment.»
DOCTOR: «But you aren't a patient of mine, are you?»
MR RICHARDS: «No, I'm not, but my aunt was and I'm her heir.»

I want to thank you for your wonderful treatment, quiero darle las gracias por su maravilloso tratamiento. ‖ *to thank* = agradecer, dar las gracias.

21

Expecting some guests to tea.
MRS MURRAY: «Why aren't you putting any saucers under the cups, Betsy?»
MAID: «Because people never drink from them.»

expecting some guests to tea, esperando a algunos invitados a tomar el té.
because people never drink from them, porque la gente nunca bebe en ellos.
 Nótese la preposición *from*. ∥ *never* va entre el sujeto y el verbo.

22

OFFICE BOSS (to secretary): «Why don't you answer the phone?
SECRETARY: «Because it's always for you.»

office boss, jefe de oficina.
why don't you answer the phone? ¿por qué no contesta usted al teléfono? ∥ *don't* se emplea en frases interrogativas negativas.

23

TOURIST (to park attendant): «Does this tree belong to the coniferous family?»
PARK ATTENDANT: «No, sir, it belongs to the Town Council.»

park attendant, guarda del parque.
does this tree belong to the coniferous family? ¿pertenece este árbol a la familia de las coníferas?
the Town Council, el Ayuntamiento.

24

MR WILLIAMSON: «Do you ever disagree with your wife?»
MR BUTLER: «Very often, but she doesn't know it.»

do you ever disagree with your wife? ¿está usted alguna vez en desacuerdo con su mujer? || *ever* se usa en frases interrogativas con la idea de «alguna vez».

25

At an asylum
FIRST MADMAN: «Why don't elephants do military service?»
SECOND MADMAN: «Because they don't have an index finger to press the rifle trigger.»

why don't elephants do military service? ¿por qué los elefantes no hacen el servicio militar? Nótese la omisión del artículo determinado delante de *elephants* y también delante de la expresión *military service*.
index finger, dedo índice.

26

MURIEL: «You say that carrots are very good for the eyesight, but I'm not quite convinced.»
MAVIS: «Well, the proof that carrots are good for the eyesight is that rabbits never wear glasses.»

but I'm not quite convinced, pero no estoy completamente convencida.
rabbits never wear glasses, los conejos nunca llevan gafas. Obsérvese la omisión del artículo determinado delante de *rabbits*, ya que se trata de una generalización. || *never* va entre el sujeto y el verbo. || *wear* significa «llevar puesto» (una prenda o gafas).

27

At the arithmetic class.
TEACHER: «Suppose you have six apples and your sister takes five of them. What are you left with?»
PUPIL: «The smallest one.»

suppose you have six apples, supón que tienes seis manzanas. || *to suppose* = suponer.
your sister takes, tu hermana coge. El verbo lleva «s» porque se trata de la tercera persona del singular del presente.
what are you left with? ¿con cuántas te quedas? Literalmente: «¿con qué te quedas?»

28

FIRST TENANT: «Does your roof always leak?»
SECOND TENANT: «Oh, no, not always. Only when it rains.»

does your roof always leak? ¿tiene siempre goteras su tejado? || *to leak* = gotear. || *always* va entre el sujeto y el verbo.

29

BOSS (to insurance agent): «I want to insure all the furniture in this office except the clock.»
INSURANCE AGENT: «Why not the clock?»
BOSS: «Because nobody takes their eyes off it.»

insurance agent, agente de seguros.
all the furniture in this office, todo el mobiliario de esta oficina. Nótese el uso de *in* en este caso.
because nobody takes their eyes off it, porque nadie aparta los ojos de él. Hay que observar el uso de *their* (plural) al referirse a *nobody* (singular). || *to take off* = quitar, apartar.

30

LANDLADY: «I don't allow noisy people in this house. Have you got any children or a dog or a radio?»
PROSPECTIVE TENANT: «No, I haven't, and when I want to gargle I get into a cupboard and close the door.»

I don't allow noisy people in this house, no permito que la gente haga ruido en esta casa. Literalmente: «no permito (que haya) gente ruidosa en esta casa». || *noise* = ruido; *noisy* = ruidoso, a. || *don't* se usa en frases negativas, excepto en la tercera persona del singular del presente.
I get into a cupboard, me meto en un armario. || *to get into* = meterse en, entrar en. || *into* se emplea cuando se menciona el lugar, en este caso: *a cupboard*.

31

MR ANDREWS: «My daughter is at the perfect age now.»
MR WHITE: «What do you mean by the perfect age?»
MR ANDREWS: «Well, she's too old to cry during the night and too young to ask me for money.»

what do you mean by the perfect age? ¿qué quieres decir con la perfecta edad? Hay que notar la preposición *by* con el verbo *to mean* (querer decir).

too old to cry during the night, demasiado mayor para llorar por la noche. ‖ *during* = durante. ‖ *old* = viejo, a.

too young to ask me for money, demasiado joven para pedirme dinero. ‖ *to ask* = preguntar. ‖ *to ask somebody for something,* pedir algo a alguien. Nótese el orden de las palabras.

32

MR COOPER (to psychiatrist): «Well, to begin with, let me tell you that I lead a very happy life. I have a very pretty wife. I live in a comfortable flat in the centre of the town. I have a cottage at the seaside. I have a Rolls Royce. My four children go to very good schools.»

PSYCHIATRIST: «Well, what's your problem, then?

MR COOPER: «My problem is that I only earn 100 pounds a month.»

to begin with, para empezar.

I lead a very happy life, llevo una vida muy feliz. ‖ *to lead* = llevar (buena o mala vida).

III   IMPERATIVO
(IMPERATIVE)

33

MAID: «I'm not interested in the job, ma'am.»
MISTRESS: «Why not?»
MAID: «Because you have thirteen children.»
MISTRESS: «Well, don't say you're superstitious.»

I'm not interested in the job, no me interesa el trabajo. Literalmente: «no estoy interesada en el trabajo».
don't say you're superstitious, no diga que es usted supersticiosa. El imperativo negativo se forma anteponiendo *don't* al verbo sin *to* delante.

34

TEACHER: «Pam, tell me the simple present of the verb "to walk".»
PAM (very slowly): «I walk... you walk... he walks...»
TEACHER: «A bit faster, please.»
PAM: «She runs, we run, they run...».

tell me the simple present of the verb «to walk», dime el presente de indicativo del verbo «to walk» (andar). El imperativo se forma con el infinitivo del verbo sin *to;* así *to tell* = decir; *tell* = di (tú), diga (usted).

a bit faster, un poquito más deprisa. ‖ *a bit* se emplea muy corrientemente en vez de la expresión *a little.*

35

At the ticket office.
MAN (to clerk, handing him a five-pound note): «Give me a return ticket to Windsor, please.»
CLERK: «Change at Slough.»
MAN: «Oh, no, I want my change here and now.»

ticket office, taquilla.
handing him a five-pound note, entregándole un billete de cinco libras. ‖ *to hand* = entregar; *hand* = mano.
return ticket, billete de ida y vuelta.
change at Slough, trasbordo en Slough. ‖ *change* también significa «cambio», de ahí el chiste.
here and now, aquí y ahora.

36

VISITOR: «Oh, don't trouble to see me to the door, Mr Jones.»
MR JONES: «It's no trouble at all. It's a pleasure.»

don't trouble to see me to the door, no se moleste en acompañarme hasta la puerta. ‖ *to see somebody to the door,* acompañar a alguien a la puerta.
it's no trouble at all, no es ninguna molestia. ‖ En la nota anterior aparece *trouble* como verbo: *don't trouble* y en la nota presente, *trouble* actúa de sustantivo: *it's no trouble.*

37

WIFE: «Let's speak face to face.»
HUSBAND: «Face to face? then, take your make up off!»

let's speak face to face, hablemos cara a cara.
take your make up off! ¡quítate el maquillaje! ‖ *take off* = quitar (se). ‖ Nótese la colocación de la partícula *off* después del objeto directo.

38

In the middle of a battle.
CAPTAIN (to major): «Sir, we're out of ammunition. There isn't a single cartridge left.»
MAJOR (shouting): «Then, cease fire!»

sir, we're out of ammunition, mi comandante, se nos ha acabado la munición.
 Nótese la palabra *sir,* en vez de «mi comandante», «mi capitán», etc.
there isn't a cartridge left, no queda ni un solo cartucho.
cease fire! ¡alto el fuego! ‖ *to cease* = cesar.

IV PRETERITO INDEFINIDO *(SIMPLE PAST)*.

USO DEL AUXILIAR *DID*.

PRETERITO IMPERFECTO *(PAST CONTINUOUS)*.

VERBOS REGULARES E IRREGULARES

39

In class.
TEACHER: «All the animals in Noah's Ark went in pairs.»
PATRICK: «That's not quite true, sir.»
TEACHER: «Why?»
PATRICK: «Because the worms went in apples!»

Noah's Ark, Arca de Noé. El chiste reside en que *pairs* (pares, parejas) se pronuncia igual que *pears* (peras). ‖ *went* es el pasado de *go* (ir).

40

At an asylum.
FIRST MADMAN: «What are you looking for?»
SECOND MADMAN: «I'm looking for a five-pound note.»
FIRST MADMAN: «Where did you lose it?»
SECOND MADMAN: «In the dining-room.»
FIRST MADMAN: «Then, why are you looking for it here in the bedroom?»
SECOND MADMAN: «Because there's more light here.»

I'm looking for a five-pound note, estoy buscando un billete de cinco libras. ‖ *to look* = mirar; *to look for* = buscar.
where did you lose it? ¿dónde lo perdiste? La forma interrogativa del pasado se forma con el auxiliar *did* y el infinitivo del verbo en cuestión: *lose* (perder).

41

FRED: «Did your wife give you a hiding when you went home late last Monday?»
ROY: «Well, err, yes, but I had to have my front teeth out one day or another anyhow.»

well, err... bien, es que... ‖ *err* se emplea al pensar lo que se va a decir.
I had to have my front teeth out, tenía que quitarme los dientes de delante. Literalmente: «Yo tenía que tener mis dientes de delante fuera.»

42

In an English class.
STUDENT (to his teacher): «What does *why* mean?»
TEACHER: «¿Por qué?»
STUDENT: «Well, I just wanted to know.»

I just wanted to know, solamente quería saberlo. ‖ El pasado de un verbo irregular se forma añadiendo *ed* al infinitivo: *I want,* yo quiero; *I wanted,* yo quería, quise.

43

The five o'clock train arrived at the station on time. The station master was so pleased that he decided to give the engine-driver a cigar.
—«Well done! Here's a cigar for you, for having arrived on time.»
—«Thank, you, sir», said the engine-driver, «but this is yesterday's train.»

well done! ¡bien hecho!
for having arrived on time, por haber llegado puntualmente.
he decided to give the engine-driver a cigar, decidió dar un puro al maquinista.
  ‖ El pasado de un verbo regular que termine en «e» se forma añadiendo «d» al infinitivo: *I decide,* yo decido; *I decided,* yo decidí.
but this is yesterday's train, pero este es el tren de ayer. Nótese el genitivo sajón con un adverbio de tiempo.

44

GAMEKEEPER (to angler): «Didn't you read that sign over there? NO FISHING IN THESE GROUNDS.»
ANGLER: «But I'm not fishing in the grounds. I'm fishing in the water.»

didn't you read that sign over there? ¿no leyó ese cartel de ahí? ‖ La forma interrogativa-negativa de un verbo en pasado se hace colocando delante el auxiliar *didn't.*
no fishing in these grounds, se prohíbe pescar en estos terrenos. Nótese la fórmula *no* + gerundio. ‖ Otro ejemplo: *no ball playing,* se prohíbe jugar a la pelota.

45

ROBERT: «How did you get that bump on your head?»
ALBERT: «Did you see that beam when you were going down the basement stairs?»
ROBERT: «Yes.»
ALBERT: «Well, I didn't.»

how did you get that bump on your head? ¿cómo te hiciste ese chichón en la cabeza? Literalmente: «¿cómo conseguiste...?».

46

On the first day at school.
SCHOOL MASTER: «Why are you crying, Jimmy?»
JIMMY: «Because my father said this morning that I've got to be here till I'm fourteen.»
SCHOOL MASTER: «Well, I've got to be here till I'm seventy and I don't complain.»

my father said this morning that I've got to be here till I'm fourteen, mi padre dijo esta mañana que tengo que estar aquí hasta que cumpla catorce años. ‖ *said,* pasado de *say* (decir).

I've got to be here, tengo que estar aquí. También *I have to be here till I'm fourteen,* hasta que tenga o hasta que cumpla catorce años. Nótese el verbo *to be* en inglés: *till I'm...*

47

At a restaurant.
The waiter took a long time to come between courses. The customer got angry and when the waiter eventually came, he said:
—«I say, why these long intervals?»
—«They aren't intervals, sir. They're noodles», replied the waiter.

the waiter took a long time to come between courses. El camarero tardaba mucho en venir entre un plato y otro. ‖ *took,* pasado de *take* (tomar). ‖ *took a long time,* tardaba (tomaba) mucho tiempo. ‖ *between courses,* literalmente: «entre platos».
eventually, finalmente. No es «eventualmente».
I say, oiga.

48

One day Mr and Mrs Davis went to the zoo. When they got to the kangaroo enclosure, Mrs Davis asked her husband:
—«What are those?»
—«They're kangaroos, natives of Australia.»
—«Natives of Australia?» said Mrs Davis sobbing. «To think our daughter married one of them!»

when they got to the kangaroo enclosure, cuando llegaron al recinto de los canguros. ‖ *got,* pasado de *get.* ‖ *to get to* = llegar a.
to think our daughter married one of them! ¡Pensar que nuestra hija se casó con uno de ellos!

49

IAN: «Did you go to see the doctor about your loss of memory?»
ANDREW: «Yes.»
IAN: «And what did he tell you?»
ANDREW: «He told me to pay him in advance.»

he told me to pay him in advance, me dijo que le pagara por adelantado. Esta construcción es muy corriente y se usa con verbos de mandato: *tell, order;* deseo: *want, wish;* ruego: *ask, beg.* Otros ejemplos: *I want you to come at once,* quiero que vengas enseguida. Obsérvese que equivale a un subjuntivo en español.

50

MOTHER: «Willie, ten minutes ago there were two cakes in the fridge and now there's only one. How's that?»
WILLIE: «Well, I didn't see the second one, mum.»

ten minutes ago, hace diez minutos.
I didn't see the second one, mum, no vi el segundo, mamá. ‖ *one* está en puesto de la palabra *cake.* ‖ El negativo de una frase en pasado se forma colocando *didn't* entre el sujeto y el verbo.

51

AUNT: «How did you get that black eye, Joey?»
JOEY: «Defending a boy.»
AUNT: «Who?»
JOEY: «Me.»

how did you get that black eye? ¿cómo es que tienes ese ojo negro? Literalmente: «¿cómo conseguiste ese ojo negro?»
Joey significa «Pepito».

52

DAVE: «Did you hear about old Tom?»
NED: «No, what happened to him?»
DAVE: «He fell dead at the pub door yesterday.»
NED: «Was he going in or coming out?»
DAVE: «He was going in.»
NED: «What bad luck!»

did you hear about old Tom? ¿has tenido noticias del viejo (amigo) Tom? || *to hear about* = oír acerca de.
he fell dead at the pub door yesterday, cayó muerto a la puerta de la taberna ayer. || *fell* es el pasado de *fall* (caer).
going in, entrando; *coming out,* saliendo.

53

SAMMY: «When I first smoked a cigarette I got terrible pains in my stomach.»
CECIL: «Well, when I first smoked a cigarette I got terrible pains all over my body.»
SAMMY: «How extraordinary! Why was that?»
CECIL: «My father gave me an awful beating.»

I got terrible pains in my stomach, me dolió el estómago terriblemente. Literalmente: «tuve terribles dolores en mi estómago».
all over my body, por todo el cuerpo.
awful beating, tremenda paliza.

54

Ted handed a letter to the clerk at the post office and said:
—«Please put a stamp on this envelope.»

The clerk gave a stamp to Ted and said to him:
—«Put it on yourself.»

Ted was very surprised, but he put the stamp on his forehead and went away.

Ted handed a letter to the clerk at the post office, Ted entregó una carta al empleado de correos.

put it on yourself, ponlo tú mismo. También puede querer decir «ponlo sobre ti mismo», de ahí el chiste.

he put the stamp on his forehead, él se puso el sello en la frente. ‖ *Put* es el presente y el pasado del verbo «poner». ‖ *forehead* se pronuncia ('forid).

55

A school-boy was so dirty and smelled so badly that his teacher wrote a tactful letter to his mother. The mother answered in the following way:
«Dear Mr Black,
I send my boy to school for you to teach him; not for you to smell him.»

a school-boy was so dirty and smelled so badly..., un alumno de la escuela estaba tan sucio y olía tan mal... ‖ *a school-boy* = un escolar. ‖ *to smell* = oler, puede hacer el pasado de forma regular o irregular: *smelled* o *smelt*.

I send my boy to school for you to teach him, mando a mi hijo a la escuela para que usted le enseñe. Obsérvese que el infinitivo en inglés se traduce por un subjuntivo en español.

56

HAROLD: «My brother lost his watch on the underground.»
ARTHUR: «How did that happen?»
HAROLD: «It was during the rush hour. He took it off to wind it up and put it back on somebody else's wrist.»

my brother lost his watch in the underground, mi hermano perdió el reloj en el metro. ‖ *lost* es el pasado del verbo *lose* (perder).

the rush hour, la hora punta.

he took it off to wind it up and put it back..., se lo quitó para darle cuerda y lo volvió a poner... Hay que notar tres verbos con partículas en esta frase: *took off, wind up* y *put back*.

57

LANDLADY: «Did you sleep well last night, Mr Harris?»
GUEST: «Well, the bed was a bit hard, so I got up from time to time and rested a little.»

a bit hard, un poco dura.
from time to time, de vez en cuando.
and rested a little, y descansaba un poquito.

58

PEGGY: «How did you come to marry Molly?»
DAVID: «I didn't come to marry Molly. I came to read the gas meter.»

how did you come to marry Molly? ¿cómo llegaste a casarte con M.? También puede significar: «¿cómo viniste a casarte con M.?», de ahí el chiste.

59

MRS FIELD: «How did you get that black eye?»
MRS JENKINS: «My husband came out of prison last Monday. It was his birthday and I wished him "Many happy returns".»

my husband came out of prison, mi marido salió de la prisión. ‖ *came* es el pasado de *come* (venir). ‖ *to come out of* = salir de.
many happy returns, puede significar: «que cumplas muchos» o también «muchos felices retornos (de días como éste)». La expresión completa es: *many happy returns of the day!*

60

A drunk rang Mr Johnson's door-bell at four o'clock in the morning. Mr Johnson got up from bed, opened the door, and said half asleep:
—«What on earth do you want at this time?»
—«Are you Mr Webster?» asked the drunk.
—«No, I'm not», shouted Mr Johnson.
—«Well, if you aren't Mr Webster, why did you open the door?» replied the drunk and went away.

and said half asleep, y dijo medio dormido. Nótese la omisión del pronombre *he* ya que el sujeto, *Mr Johnson*, está expresado en la primera frase a la que le siguen dos más, la segunda separada por coma y la tercera por la palabra *and*.
what on earth...? ¿qué demonios...? Literalmente: «¿qué sobre la tierra...?»

61

At a party.
MR KELLY: «Who is that awful gossip in the corner?»
MR MASON: «My wife.»
MR KELLY: «Sorry. I made a terrible mistake.»
MR MASON: «No, the mistake was mine.»

awful gossip, tremenda cotilla.
in the corner, en el rincón.
I made a terrible mistake, he cometido una falta terrible. Literalmente: «hice una falta terrible». ll *made* es el pasado de *make* (hacer).

62

A tourist on a motor-bike is going at full speed along the road to Stratford-upon-Avon. He stops and asks a villager:
—«Where's Shakespeare's house, please?»
—«It's behind those trees over there, but there's no need to go so fast. He died many years ago.»

at full speed, a toda velocidad.
along the road, por la carretera.
over there, allí (alejado).
there's no need to go so fast, no hay necesidad de ir tan deprisa.

63

MRS GORDON: «Why did you leave your last job?»
PROSPECTIVE MAID: «Because my mistress ordered me to bath the children and I refused to.»
MRS GORDON'S CHILDREN: «Take her, Mummy. Don't let her go!»

because my mistress ordered me to bath the children and I refused to, porque mi señora me mandó (ordenó) que bañara a los niños y yo me negué. Se sobreentiende: *I refused to bath them*.
don't let her go! ¡no dejes que se vaya!

64

One day a drunk got on a double-decker bus. He went up to the top deck and rushed down the stairs again at once. The conductor asked him:
—«What's wrong?»
—«I don't want to go on this bus. There's no driver», said the drunk getting off the bus.

a double-decker bus, un autobús de dos pisos.
the top deck, el piso de arriba.
and rushed down the stairs, y bajó corriendo las escaleras.
Nótense estos dos verbos: *to get on* = subirse (a un vehículo); *to get off* = apearse (de un vehículo).

65

ELIZABETH: «I hear your boyfriend gave you a beautiful pearl for you birthday.»
KATE: «Well, not exactly; he gave me an oyster and said: "I wish you good luck".»

I hear your boyfriend..., tengo entendido que tu novio... Está omitida la conjunción *that: I hear that your boyfriend...* Es corriente la omisión de esta conjunción delante de oraciones sustantivas con oficio de objeto.
gave es el pasado de *give* (dar).

66

UNCLE: «Why did you have to leave school, Roger?»
ROGER: «Illness.»
UNCLE: «Really? What was wrong?»
ROGER: «The teacher said that he was sick of me.»

to leave school, dejar la escuela (los estudios). Compárese con *to leave the school*, dejar la escuela (salir del edificio).
the teacher said that he was sick of me, el profesor dijo que estaba harto de mí. || *sick* también significa «enfermo», de ahí el chiste. || Asimismo: *the teacher said he was sick of me*, omitiendo la conjunción *that*.

67

Dolly and Leslie are dancing.
LESLIE: «The floor is rather slippery, isn't it?»
DOLLY: «The floor isn't slippery. It's my shoes. I polished them this morning.»

rather slippery, bastante resbaladizo. || El adverbio *rather* se suele usar con adjetivos desfavorables.
it's my shoes, son mis zapatos. Nótese el pronombre *it* en este caso. La idea es: «ello es *(it is)*, (la causa es) mis zapatos.»

68

OFFICE CLERK: «What fool put this tray on my table?»
SECRETARY: «The boss.»
OFFICER CLERK: «Oh! Isn't it nice?»

what fool put...? ¿qué tonto puso...? || El verbo *put* (poner) tiene la misma forma en presente y en pasado.

69

MRS JENKINS: «My husband gave me this mink coat for my thirtieth birthday.»
MRS GREY: «It looks fine, dear. Mink wears very well.»

my husband gave me..., mi marido me regaló... Literalmente: «me dio». ‖ *gave* es el pasado de *give* (dar).

mink wears very well, el visón dura mucho. ‖ *to wear* significa «llevar puesto» (una prenda) y también «durar» (ropa).

70

One day a woman went into a shop to buy a shirt for her husband. She chose a blue one. The shop-assistant asked her if she wanted another.

—«Another shirt?», said the woman in surprise. «But I only have one husband.»

a woman went into a shop, una mujer entró en una tienda. ‖ *into* se emplea al mencionar el lugar donde se entra. Compárese con *she went in*, ella entró (sin decir dónde).

she chose a blue one, eligió una azul. ‖ *chose* es el pasado del verbo *choose* (elegir). ‖ El pronombre *one* se emplea para no repetir el sustantivo *shirt*.

71

HERBERT: «I don't know what Larry spends his money on. Last Saturday he had no money and today he has no money either.»
JONATHAN: «Did he try to borrow some from you?»
HERBERT: «No, I tried to borrow some from him.»

I don't know what Larry spends his money on, no sé en qué gasta el dinero Larry. Nótese la colocación de la preposición *on* al final de la oración. ‖ Obsérvese el uso de *his*.

and today he has no money either, y hoy tampoco tiene dinero. ‖ *either* significa «tampoco» en una oración negativa.

GRAMMAR AND HUMOUR

72

At supper.
HUSBAND: «Mushrooms again?»
WIFE: «You're very hard to please, dear. The day before yesterday you liked mushrooms; yesterday you liked mushrooms, but today you say you don't like mushrooms.»

you're very hard to please, eres muy difícil de contentar. || *hard* significa «duro» y también «difícil».

73

At the hospital.
NURSE: «How do you feel today?»
PATIENT: «I feel as if I had a bump on my head.»
NURSE: «Well, err, the doctor ran out of anaesthetic towards the end of the operation.»

I feel as if I had a bump on my head, me siento como si tuviera un chichón en la cabeza. También: «como si me hubieran dado un golpe en la cabeza».
the doctor ran out of anaesthetic, al doctor se le acabó la anestesia. || El verbo *run*, pasado *ran*, significa «correr». || *run out of* quiere decir «agotarse, acabarse» (algo).

V PRETERITO PERFECTO (PRESENT PERFECT). VERBOS REGULARES E IRREGULARES

74

INTERVIEWER (to ninety-year-old woman): «Have you spent all your life on this farm?»
NINETY-YEAR-OLD WOMAN: «Not yet.»

ninety-year-old woman, mujer de noventa años. Hay que notar *year* en singular. *have you spent...?,* ¿ha pasado usted...? El pretérito perfecto (present perfect) se forma con el auxiliar *have/has* y el participio pasado del verbo en cuestión. ǁ *spent* es el participio pasado de *spend* (pasar, gastar).

75

At a restaurant.
CUSTOMER: «I've asked for a pork chop a hundred times.»
WAITER (aloud to the cook): «A hundred pork chops for this gentleman, please!»

I've asked for a pork chop, he pedido una chuleta de cerdo. ǁ *I've* es la contracción de *I have.* ǁ *ask* = preguntar; *ask for* = pedir. ǁ El participio pasado de los verbos regulares se forma añadiendo «-ed» al verbo: *ask—asked.*

76

At a hotel in the country.
GUEST: «You've charged me ten pounds for keeping my car in the garage for only one night. I think it's far too much.»
HOTEL KEEPER: «Well, sir, the explanation is that it is a horse stable, not a garage, and your car is 80 horse power.»

you've charged me ten pounds for keeping my car in the garage, me ha cobrado usted diez libras por guardarme el coche en el garaje. ‖ El participio pasado de los verbos regulares que terminan por «e» se forma añadiendo «-d»: *charge—charged*.
and your car is 80 horse power, y su coche tiene 80 caballos.

77

FATHER: «Oh!, Frankie, you've lost three of your teeth! I bet you've been fighting that big boy again!»
FRANKIE: «Oh!, no, daddy. I haven't lost my teeth. I've got them in my pocket.»

I bet you've been fighting that big boy again!, apuesto a que te has pegado otra vez con ese chico tan grandullón. ‖El verbo *you've been fighting* está en forma continua para indicar una acción repetida. Literalmente: «te has estado pegando...». ‖ *you've* es la contracción de *you have*.
lost es el participio pasado de *lose* (perder).
I've got them, los tengo.

78

RICHARD: «I hear you've been to Spain. Did you have any difficulty with your Spanish?»
FRANK: «No, but the Spaniards did.»

I hear you've been to Spain, tengo entendido que has estado en España. ‖ La forma *I hear*, literalmente «oigo», es muy corriente en inglés y se usa con la idea de «he oído», «me han dicho», «tengo entendido».

79

Mrs Williamson: «The sideboard is covered with dust, Molly. It's been there for at least three weeks.»
Maid: «I've nothing to do with that, ma'am. I've only been here for ten days.»

covered with dust, cubierto de polvo. Nótese la diferencia de preposición entre el inglés y el español.
it's been there for at least three weeks, hace que está ahí por lo menos tres semanas. Obsérvese que el presente español: «está» acompañado de la palabra «hace» se traduce en inglés por el *present perfect*, literalmente: «ha estado ahí...». De la misma manera: *I've only been here for ten days*, hace sólo diez días que estoy aquí.

80

On the telephone:
—«Is that the Telephone Company?»
—«No, this is the Electricity Company.»
—«Oh, sorry, I've picked up the iron instead of the receiver.»

I've picked up the iron instead of the receiver, he cogido la plancha en vez del auricular.

81

Mrs Thompson: «I've been to four doctors and each has given a completely different diagnosis.»
Mrs Richards: «How strange! Didn't they agree on anything?»
Mrs Thompson: «Oh, yes, they agreed on their fees. They all charged me ten pounds for each visit.»

I've been to four doctors, he ido a cuatro médicos.
given es el participio pasado de *give* (dar).
didn't they agree on anything?, ¿no estaban de acuerdo en algo?
they all charged me, todos me cobraron. Nótese la colocación de *all* entre el pronombre y el verbo.

GRAMMAR AND HUMOUR

82

The Browns have invited the Blakes to tea. Mrs Brown offers them some fruit cake. Mrs Blake tastes it and says:
—«This cake is delicious, dear. Did you buy it yourself?»

the Browns have invited the Blakes to tea, los Brown han invitado a los Blake a tomar el té.
fruit cake, pastel de frutas.
did you buy it yourself?, ¿lo compraste tú misma?

83

In a maternity home.
NURSE (calling Mr Harris): «You have a fine boy, Mr Harris.»
MR DAVIS (complaining): «I protest. I've been here for two hours. I came before him.»

I've been here for two hours, hace dos horas que estoy aquí. Véase 79.
came es el pasado del verbo *come* (venir).

84

Two friends meet in the street.
FRED: «Hallo, Robert, how's things?»
ROBERT: «Well, I'm all right. At the moment I'm selling cars.»
FRED: «How many have you sold?»
ROBERT: «Well, so far I've sold my Mini.»

two friends meet in the street, dos amigos se encuentran en la calle.
how's things? ¿cómo van las cosas? (Forma coloquial).
at the moment, en la actualidad.
so far, hasta ahora.

85

Two philosophers are having a philosophical talk.
FIRST PHILOSOPHER: «I've discovered that there are many more important things in life than money.»
SECOND PHILOSOPHER: «Oh, yes, you're quite right, but the only snag is that you need money to buy them.»

a philosophical talk, una charla filosófica. || talk puede ser sustantivo: «charla» y verbo: «charlar».
you're quite right, tiene toda la razón. || to be right = tener razón. Lo contrario es to be wrong.
the only snag, la única pega.

86

MRS BOSWELL: «My husband doesn't understand me; does yours?»
MRS COLE: «I don't know. He's never spoken to me about you.»

does yours? ¿y el tuyo? Se sobreentiende: «¿te entiende a ti?».
he's never es la contracción de he has never.
spoken es el participio pasado del verbo speak (hablar).

87

FRIEND: «Why does your dog run into a corner of the room every time the doorbell sounds?»
DOG OWNER: «Haven't you noticed it's a boxer?»

... *every time the doorbell sounds?* ¿... cada vez que suena la campana (o timbre) de la puerta?
boxer significa «boxeador», además de designar una raza de perros.

88

At a tea-shop.
CUSTOMER: «Waiter, please bring me two lumps of sugar for my tea.»
WAITER: «But you've already put in eight lumps, sir.»
CUSTOMER: «Yes, I know, but they have all dissolved.»

but you've already put in eight lumps, pero usted ya se ha puesto ocho terrones. Nótese la colocación de *already* entre el verbo auxiliar: *have* y el principal: *put*. ‖ *put in* = meter.
they have all dissolved, todos se han disuelto. Hay que notar la colocación de *all* entre el verbo auxiliar: *have* y el principal: *dissolved*.

89

ANTHONY: «Paul is so lazy that I don't know how tall he is.»
PEGGY: «What do you mean? What's the connection between his laziness and his height?»
ANTHONY: «Well, I've never seen him standing up.»

... *so lazy that I don't know how tall he is,* ... tan vago que no sé cómo es de alto.
what's the connection between his laziness and his height? ¿qué tiene que ver su pereza con su estatura? Literalmente: «¿cuál (qué) es la conexión entre su pereza y su altura?».
standing up, de pie.

90

At a restaurant.
CUSTOMER: «I see you've taken on a new person to do the washing up.»
OWNER: «How did you know?»
CUSTOMER: «Well, the finger-prints on the plates and glasses are different now.»

I see you've taken on a new person, veo que han contratado a otra persona. ‖ *a new person,* literalmente: «una nueva persona».
to do the washing up, para que friegue los cacharros.
finger-prints, huellas dactilares.

91

PAULINE: «Look, Susie, my husband has given me this fur coat as a present for our wedding anniversary.»
SUSIE: «How lovely! He has an excellent taste.»
PAULINE: «Oh, no, he didn't choose it. He doesn't know anything about it yet.»

my husband has given me, mi marido me ha dado. ‖ *given* es el participio pasado de *give* (dar).
wedding anniversary, aniversario de boda.
how lovely! ¡qué bonito!
he doesn't know anything about it yet, todavía no sabe nada (de ello). ‖ *anything* significa «nada» en una frase negativa.

92

At a hospital.
NURSE (to man with his head and arm bandaged up): «Are you married?»
MAN: «Yes, I am, but this time I've had a car accident.»

bandaged up, vendados.
I've had a car accident, he tenido un accidente de coche.

93

In the corridor of a hospital.
FIRST NURSE: «Why are you so angry, Vicky?»
SECOND NURSE: «Because I've just broken off my engagement to Doctor Harris.»
FIRST NURSE: «That's not a reason to be angry.»
SECOND NURSE: «Isn't it? He had the cheek to send me a bill for twenty-five visits.»

I've just broken off my engagement to doctor Harris, acabo de romper mi compromiso con el doctor H. ‖ *Just* se usa entre el verbo auxiliar *have* y el verbo principal *broken off,* con la idea de «acabar de (hacer algo)». ‖ *broken* es el participio pasado del verbo *break* (romper).

94

HUSBAND: «You are very wasteful, dear. That electric fire has been on all evening and it isn't very cold today.»
WIFE: «There's no need to worry. It isn't ours. I borrowed it from our next-door neighbour this morning.»

that electric fire has been on all evening, esa estufa eléctrica ha estado encendida toda la tarde.
there's no need to worry, no hay por qué preocuparse. ‖ *there's* es la contracción de *there is.* ‖ *need* = necesidad. ‖ *to worry* = preocuparse.
next-door neighbour, vecino de al lado.

95

At court.
JUDGE: «Why do you say this man was drunk?»
WITNESS: «Well, he went up to a letter box, put a coin in the slot and looking up at Big Ben, exclaimed, "Oh. I've lost one stone in a quarter of an hour!".»

at court, en el tribunal de justicia.
he went up to a letter box, se acercó a un buzón. ‖ *to go up to,* acercarse a.
and looking up at Big Ben, y mirando (hacia arriba) al Big Ben.
I've lost, he perdido. ‖ el verbo «perder» es *to lose, lost, lost.*

96

After seven years' absence in Australia, Sean returns home and finds his brother Ian with a very long beard.
SEAN: «Why have you grown such a long beard, Ian?»
IAN: «Because you took the razor with you when you went to Australia.»

after seven years' absence, después de una ausencia de siete años. Obsérvese el genitivo sajón con una expresión de tiempo.

why have you grown such a long beard? ¿por qué te has dejado crecer una barba tan larga? || *to grow,* crecer, cultivar. También «dejarse crecer» (el bigote, la barba).

you took the razor with you, te llevaste la maquinilla de afeitar.

grown es el participio pasado de *grow* (crecer); *took* es el pasado de *take* (tomar); *went* es el pasado de *go* (ir, irse).

97

BOY: «What are you fishing for?»
ANGLER: «I'm fishing for trout.»
BOY: «How many have you caught?»
ANGLER: «None yet.»
BOY: «Then how do doy know you're fishing for trout?»

what are you fishing for? ¿qué pescas (estás pescando)? || En preguntas que comienzan por las palabras interrogativas *what, where, how* precedidas de una preposición, ésta pasa al final de la frase. Otros ejemplos: *where are you from?* ¿de dónde eres?, *how long have you lived here for?* ¿cuánto tiempo hace que vives aquí?

I'm fishing for trout, pesco (estoy pescando) truchas. *Trout* no tiene plural, de igual manera *sheep* y *salmon,* entre otras.

how many have you caught? ¿cuántas has pescado (cogido)? || *caught* es el participio pasado de *catch* (coger, atrapar).

98

Mrs Purcell caught a cold and drank a glass of brandy. A little later she went to say good night to her small daughter and kissed her. Her daughter then said to her:
—«Mummy, you've been using daddy's perfume, haven't you?»

Mrs Purcell caught a cold, la Sra. P. cogió un resfriado. ‖ *caught* es el pasado de *catch* (atrapar). ‖ *cold,* frío, resfriado.
a little later, un poco más tarde.
you've been using daddy's perfume, haven't you?, has usado el perfume de papá, ¿verdad? Literalmente: «has estado usando...».

99

On a London bus.
DRUNK (to man in uniform): «A ticket to Marble Arch, please.»
MAN IN UNIFORM: «I'm not the conductor. I'm an R.A.F. officer.»
DRUNK: «Heavens! I've got on a bomber!»

I'm not the conductor, no soy el cobrador. ‖ No se confunda: *conductor,* cobrador (de un vehículo); *driver,* conductor.
I've got on a bomber! ¡me he subido a un bombardero! ‖ la «b» es muda en *bomber.*

VI PLUSCUAMPERFECTO
(PLUPERFECT)

100

At a wedding reception.
TIM (looking at the bride in surprise): «You don't look tired at all!»
BRIDE: «Should I? Why?»
TIM: «Well, Mummy just said that you'd been running after Henry Smith for six years.»

wedding reception, recepción que se da después de una boda.
looking at the bride in surprise, mirando a la novia sorprendido.
at all, en absoluto.
should I? ¿debería yo (parecer cansada)?
mummy just said that you'd been running after H. S. for six years, mamá dijo hace un momento (*just* da la idea de «justamente», «hace un momento») que usted había estado corriendo tras H. S. durante seis años. ‖ El pluscuamperfecto indica un tiempo pasado: *had been running*, anterior a otro pasado: *mummy just said*.
you'd been = you had been.

VII FUTURO *(FUTURE)*

101

Elmer is a big eater. just this morning for breakfast he ate five pears, two apples and six oranges. His mother said:
—«Elmer, you eat a lot. One of these days you will burst.»
—«Mummy, give me that cake and stand aside», said the boy with his mouth full.

big eater, comilón.
just this morning, precisamente esta mañana.
ate, pasado de *eat* (comer).
you will burst, reventarás. ‖ Con el auxiliar *will* entre el sujeto y el verbo se forma el futuro.
stand aside, apártate.
with his mouth full, con la boca llena.

102

At the hospital.
DOCTOR (to patient): «Don't worry. I'll have you out of here in a week's time one way or another.»

don't worry, no se preocupe.
I'll have you out of here, le haré que salga de aquí. Literalmente: «le tendré fuera de aquí». ‖ *I'll* es la contracción de *I will*.
one way or another, de un modo o de otro. ‖ *way* = camino, manera, modo.

103

One day there was a man going along the street with his pockets full of silver objects. As the man looked very suspicious, a police officer asked him:
—«How do you account for having your pockets full of silver objects?»
—«Well, officer», replied the man, «you won't believe me, but the thing is that I haven't got a cupboard at home.»

along the street, por la calle.
as the man looked very suspicious, como el hombre parecía muy sospechoso.
 ‖ *look* significa «mirar» y también «parecer», cuando va seguido de un adjetivo.
how do you account for having...? ¿cómo explica el tener...?
you won't believe me, no me creerá. ‖ *won't* se usa para la forma negativa del futuro y es la contracción de *will not.*

104

After the examination the teacher is correcting the exercises.
—«I want to be fair this time, Simon, I'll give you a ten for this essay: Five for your father and five for you.»

I want to be fair this time, quiero ser justo esta vez.
I'll give you a ten for this essay, te daré (un) diez por esta redacción.

105

BERYL: «My wife is always telling me she's going to leave me.»
MICHAEL: «That's all you'll ever get— promises!»

she's going to leave me, ella me va a dejar. ‖ La forma *going to* precedida del verbo *to be* indica un futuro de intención.
that's all you'll ever get, eso es todo lo que conseguirás. ‖ *ever* significa «alguna vez».

106

FORTUNE-TELLER (looking at a glass ball): «Somebody very near you will certainly be greatly disappointed.»
MR POTTER: «Oh, yes, it's you. I've forgotten to bring my money with me.»

will certainly be greatly disappointed, ciertamente estará muy decepcionado. ‖ *greatly* = en gran manera.
I've forgotten, se me ha olvidado. ‖ *forgotten* es el participio pasado de *forget* (olvidar).

107

WIFE: «I've got to go shopping now. I'll be back at about five.»
HUSBAND: «Where's my lunch?»'
WIFE: «You'll find it on page 45 of the cookery book, dear.»

I've got to go shopping now, tengo que ir de compras ahora.
I'll be back, volveré.
you'll find it, lo encontrarás.
cookery book, libro de cocina.

108

At a restaurant.
CUSTOMER: «This wine isn't worth much.»
WAITER: «You won't say that when I give you the bill.»

this wine isn't worth much, este vino no vale mucho. || *to be worth* = valer.
when I give you the bill, cuando le dé la cuenta.

109

Ben is in bed. His mother is in the kitchen.
BEN (shouting): «Mummy, bring me a comic.»
MOTHER: «No, go to sleep, Ben!»
   Two minutes later.
BEN: «Mummy, bring me a comic.»
MOTHER (angrily): «Ben go to sleep or I'll give you a hiding.»
BEN: «Mummy, when you come to give me a hiding, please bring me a comic.»

go to sleep, duérmete. Literalmente: «vete a dormir». Distíngase entre *to go to sleep,* dormirse, quedarse dormido y *to go to bed,* irse a dormir.
I'll give you a hiding, te daré una paliza.

110

STEPHEN: «So you're going to marry Graham instead of me? Well, I want to have a talk with him. Where does he live?»
KATHERINE: «You aren't going to do him any harm, are you?»
STEPHEN: «Oh, no, I'm going to sell him the ring.»

so you're going to marry Graham, así que te vas a casar con Graham. Nótese el futuro que indica intención o decisión previa: *you're going to marry,* vas a casarte. Se construye con el verbo *to be* + *going to* + el verbo en cuestión, en este caso *marry.* ‖ Nótense, en este mismo texto, dos casos más: *you aren't going to do him any harm,* no le vas a hacer ningún daño; *I'm going to sell him the ring,* voy a venderle la sortija.
I want to have a talk with him, quiero tener una charla con él.

111

TENANT: «The roof is in such bad condition that the rain comes right through and I get wet. How long will this go on for?»
LANDLORD: «I don't know, I'm the owner of the house, not a weather-prophet.»

the rain comes right through, la lluvia cala. Literalmente: «la lluvia viene (pasa) precisamente a través».
and I get wet, y yo me mojo.
how long will this go on for? ¿cuánto tiempo durará? También *for* podría ir al principio: *for how long...?* Literalmente: «¿por cuánto tiempo continuará esto?» ‖ *to go on* = continuar.
weather-prophet, el que predice el tiempo.

112

At a fashion shop.
CUSTOMER: «I want to buy a scarf for my wife. It's a present for her birthday.»
SHOP-ASSISTANT: «You're going to give her a surprise, aren't you?»
CUSTOMER: «Of course, she's expecting a mink coat.»

you're going to give her a surprise, aren't you? va usted a darle una sorpresa, ¿no?
of course, desde luego.
mink coat, abrigo de visón.

113

It was the first day at school. When Molly's mother left her daughter there, there were tears in her eyes.
MOLLY: «Don't worry, mum. As soon as I learn how to read comics I'll leave school.»

when Molly's mother left her daughter there, cuando la madre de M. dejó a su hija allí. || *left* es el pasado de *leave* (dejar).
there were tears in her eyes, se le llenaron los ojos de lágrimas. Literalmente: «había lágrimas en sus ojos».
as soon as I learn, en cuanto aprenda.
I'll leave school, dejaré la escuela. Obsérvese la omisión del artículo determinado. Distíngase entre *to leave school,* dejar la escuela (los estudios) y *to leave the school,* dejar la escuela (el edificio).

114

Just before his operation, the patient took out his wallet and looked at the money inside.
DOCTOR: «That's all right. You don't need to pay me now.»
PATIENT: «I'm only going to count my money before you give me the anaesthetic.»

just before his operation, the patient took out his wallet, justamente antes de la (su) operación, el paciente sacó la cartera. || *took out* es el pasado de *take out* (sacar).
and looked at the money inside, y miró el dinero (que había) dentro.
I'm only going to count the money, sólo voy a contar el dinero. || *only* = sólo, solamente.

115

Once an elderly man was riding on a bus. He saw that from time to time the bus-driver put his hand out of the window. At last he said:
—«Driver, don't take your hand off the wheel. I'll tell you when it begins to rain.»

once an elderly man was riding on a bus, una vez un señor mayor iba en autobús. || *ride* significa «cabalgar», «montar en».
the bus-driver put his hand out of the window, el conductor sacaba la mano por la ventanilla. || *put out of* significa «sacar de».
at last, por último.
I'll tell you, le diré.

116

Just after the robbery.
FIRST THIEF: «Let's sit down and see what we've got.»
SECOND THIEF: «There's no time now. We'll see it in the papers tomorrow.»

just after the robbery, justamente después del robo.
let's sit down and see..., vamos a sentarnos para ver... Literalmente: «sentémonos y veamos...».
we'll see it, lo veremos. || *we'll* es la contracción de *we shall* o *we will*.

VIII VERBOS DEFECTIVOS O ANÓMALOS (*DEFECTIVE OR ANOMALOUS VERBS*)

117

MAYOR OF THE TOWN: «Ladies and gentlemen. I'm very pleased to give this award to our hero for performing such a dangerous rescue operation in the river. (To hero): Would you like to say anything?»
HERO: «Yes, I'd like to know who gave me the push!»

I'm very pleased, me alegra mucho. Literalmente: «estoy muy complacido».
for performing, por llevar a cabo.
would you like? ¿le gustaría?
I'd like to know who gave me the push, me gustaría saber quién me dio el empujón. ‖ *I'd like* es la contracción de *I would like*, me gustaría. ‖ *push* como verbo es «empujar»; como sustantivo, «empujón».

118

BOBBY: «Mummy, last night I dreamt I fell into the river.»
MUMMY: «Did you? So what?»
BOBBY: «So, must I wash my face today?»

last night I dreamt I fell into the river, anoche soñé que me caí al río. ‖ *dreamt* es el pasado de *dream* (soñar). ‖ *fell* (caer, caerse). ‖ Hay que observar que está omitida la conjunción *that*, lo que es muy corriente: *I dreamt (that) I fell...*
must I wash my face today? ¿debo lavarme la cara hoy? La forma interrogativa de un verbo defectivo se hace colocando el sujeto detrás del verbo.

119

MR FISHER: «Your wife told me that you have adopted a five-year-old English orphan.»
MR GARCIA: «Yes, so when he grows up we can have free English lessons.»

a five-year-old English orphan, un huérfano inglés de cinco años. Hay que notar la colocación de las palabras.
we can have free English lessons, podemos tener lecciones de inglés gratis.

120

TEACHER (giving his students instructions about their final examination): «The examination paper consists of 50 pages, and you must complete it in one hour.»
STUDENT: «But we shan't have enough time!»
TEACHER: «Well, don't worry. You'll all be in the same boat.»
VOICE AT THE BACK OF THE CLASS: «Yes, the Titanic!»

examination paper, supuesto de examen.
you must complete it in one hour, deben hacerlo (completarlo) en una hora.
 || El verbo must se usa en este caso con sentido de obligación.
shan't es la contracción de shall not.
you'll all be in the same boat, todos estaréis en el mismo caso. Literalmente: «todos estaréis en el mismo barco».

121

YOUNG MAN: «I've come to ask for the hand of your daughter Mildred.»
MILDRED'S FATHER: «Oh, no, you must take the whole girl or nothing at all.»

you must take the whole girl or nothing at all, debes llevarte (tomar) toda la chica o nada (en absoluto). || must está empleado en este caso con la idea de obligación. *whole* (todo, toda) se emplea en vez de *all* delante de un sustantivo en singular. Otros ejemplos: *the whole book,* todo el libro; *the whole cake,* todo el pastel.

122

MRS BIXBY (to visitor): «Would you like another cake, Mrs Nixon?»
MRS NIXON: «Oh, no, thank you. I don't know how many I've eaten already.»
TEDDY: «Eleven.»

would you like another cake? ¿quiere usted otro pastel? También: «¿le gustaría otro pastel?». Esta es la fórmula corriente de ofrecer algo.
eaten es el participio pasado de *eat* (comer).

123

A man stops another man in the street and says to him:
—«How you've changed, Henry! You used to have fair hair and now you're bald. You used to be fat and now you're thin.»
—«But I'm not Henry.»
—«Oh! So you've changed your name as well!»

you used to have, solías tener. || *used*, con la idea de «soler», se emplea sólo en pasado y se pronuncia [ju:st]. Cuando esta palabra significa «usaba» se pronuncia [ju:zd]; por ejemplo: *my father used this pen*, mi padre usó esta pluma.
as well, también.

124

CHARLES: «How disgusting! I've just found a worm in this apple.»
KEN: «It would have been more disgusting to find half a worm.»

how disgusting! ¡qué asco!
I've just found, acabo de encontrar. || *found* es el participio pasado del verbo *find* (encontrar).
it would have been, habría sido.

125

A woman was driving along the road when she saw a man climbing up a telegraph pole:
—«How silly!» she exclaimed. «He must think I'm a dangerous driver.»

how silly! ¡qué tonto!
he must think I'm a dangerous driver, debe de creer que soy una conductora peligrosa. || *must*, en este caso, está empleado con la idea de suposición.

126

Annie, a twelve-year-old girl went into a shop to buy her father a tie. The shop-assistant asked what colour and design she had in mind. As Annie hesitated, the shop-asistant pointed to his own tie and said:
—«Do you think your father would like a tie like this?»
—«Oh, no. My father wants a clean one», answered Annie.

do you think your father would like a tie like this? ¿crees que a tu padre le gustaría una corbata como ésta? || *like* significa «gustar», y también «como». *would like* = gustaría. ||

my father wants a clean one, mi padre quiere una limpia. || *one* está en puesto de la palabra *tie,* para no repetir ésta en el texto.

127

TONY: «What's your baby sister's name?»
PETE: «I don't know.»
TONY: «Why don't know?»
PETE: «She can't tell us because she can't talk yet.»

baby sister, hermanita.
she can't tell us because she can't talk yet, ella no nos lo puede decir porque aún no sabe hablar. || *can't* es el negativo de *can* en forma contracta. Obsérvese que en el primer caso se ha traducido por «no puede» y en el segundo, por «no sabe».

128

Two old men in a restaurant.
FIRST OLD MAN: «I'd like a bowl of soup and a pork pie.»
SECOND OLD MAN: «I'll have a pork pie and a bowl of soup.»
WAITER: «So, two bowls of soup and two pork pies.»
FIRST OLD MAN: «Yes, but bring them in that order, please. We only have one set of false teeth.»

I'd like, quisiera, me gustaría. Es la forma corriente que se emplea para pedir algo.
a bowl of soup, un plato de sopa. || *bowl* = plato hondo.
a pork pie, una empanada o pastel de cerdo.
set of false teeth, dentadura postiza.

129

Mrs Field takes her son Timmy to the doctor.
DOCTOR: «Put out your tongue, Timmy.»
TIMMY: «No, I won't.»
DOCTOR: «Why not?»
TIMMY: «Yesterday I put out my tongue in class and the teacher hit me with a ruler.»

put out your tongue, saca la lengua.
Timmy es el diminutivo de *Timothy*, Timoteo.
I won't es la forma contracta de *I will not* y en este caso significa «no lo haré» (no quiero hacerlo).
the teacher hit me with a ruler, el profesor me pegó con una regla. || *hit* es la forma de presente, pasado y participio pasado del verbo «golpear».

130

MR COWAN: «Doctor, you certainly kept your promise when you said I'd walking again in a fortnight.»
DOCTOR: «I'm so glad. You followed my treatment to the letter, didn't you?»
MR COWAN: «Yes, doctor. And I had to sell my Mini.»

you certainly kept your promise, usted ciertamente mantuvo su promesa. || *kept* es el pasado de *keep* (guardar, mantener).
I'd be walking again, yo estaría andando de nuevo.
to the letter, al pie de la letra.

GRAMMAR AND HUMOUR

131

A tenant was playing the trumpet very late at night. The landlady interrupted him and said:
—«Don't you know there's a nursing home next door?»
—«No, I don't know that one», answered the tenant. «Can you hum a bit of it for me, please?»

don't you know there's a nursing home next door? ¿no sabe usted que hay una clínica al lado? El que toca la trompeta entiende: *don't you know «there's a nursing home next door?»* como si se tratara del título de una canción.
a bit of it, un poquito (de ello).

132

One day a motorist ran over a cat, got out of the car, and tried to find the owner of the cat to apologise. When he found him, he said:
—«Listen. I'm sorry I ran over your cat and I'd like to replace it.»
The owner of the cat replied:
—«Really? Well, get ready, then. There's a mouse in the kitchen.»

I ran over your cat, atropellé a su gato. || *ran* es el pasado del verbo *run* (correr); *run over* (atropellar).

I'd like to replace it, me gustaría (quisiera) restituirlo. También «reemplazarlo», de ahí el chiste.

133

At a party.
MR LEE: «Do you like Mozart's works?»
MEMBER OF THE NOUVEAU RICHE: «I don't know them but I must visit them one of these days.»

do you like Mozart's works? ¿le gusta las obras de Mozart? || *works* significa «obras» y también «fábrica, factoría», por ejemplo: *glass works, brick works,* de ahí el chiste.
member of the nouveau riche, nuevo rico.
I must visit them, debo visitarlo. Nótese *them* ya que se refiere a *works,* plural.
  || *must* = deber, se usa para dar idea de algo que uno debe (tiene que) hacer y no debe perderse. Otro ejemplo: *when you go to Madrid you must visit the Prado Museum,* cuando vaya a Madrid debe visitar el Museo del Prado.

134

CHARLIE: «Your brother Billy must drive very fast because they say he drives like lightning.»
STEVEN: «No, they say he drives like lightning because he's always striking trees.»

your brother Bill must drive very fast, tu hermano Bill debe de conducir muy deprisa. || *must,* en este caso, está empleado con idea de suposición.
he drives like lightning, conduce como el rayo. Nótese la omisión del artículo delante de *lightning.*
he's always striking trees, siempre está dando (golpeando) a los árboles.

135

MR ROBERTS (to doctor over the phone): «My daughter has just swallowed a 50p coin!»
DOCTOR: «Don't worry. I'll be there at once.»
As the doctor is about to leave his house, the telephone rings again.
MR ROBERTS: «There's no need for you to come, doctor. I've found another coin. Now I can buy the newspaper!»

my daughter has just swallowed a 50p coin, mi hija se acaba de tragar una moneda de 50 peniques.
as the doctor is about to leave his house, cuando el doctor está a punto de salir de casa. ‖ *to leave his house* = dejar su casa.
now I can buy the newspaper! ¡ya puedo comprar el periódico! También: «ahora puedo comprar...».

136

A man visits his doctor.
DOCTOR: «How long do you sleep every day?»
MAN: «Let me see... I sleep about four hours.»
DOCTOR: «Well, that's not enough. You should sleep more than that.»
MAN: «Oh, but I sleep for nine hours during the night too.»

how long...? ¿cuánto tiempo...?
let me see..., vamos a ver...
I sleep about four hours, duermo unas cuatro horas.
you should sleep more than that, debería usted dormir más (que eso). ‖ *should,* en este caso, da la idea de consejo.

137

At the butcher's.
CUSTOMER: «I'd like 5p's worth of bacon.»
BUTCHER: «For 5p I can only let you smell the knife.»

I'd like 5p's worth of bacon, quiero cinco peniques de tocino. || *I'd like,* quisiera, me gustaría. Esta es una fórmula muy corriente de pedir algo en una tienda. || *5p's worth of bacon,* el valor de 5 peniques de tocino.
I can only let you, sólo puedo dejarle. || *let* = dejar (permitir).

138

At a pet shop.
—«I'll buy this parrot. Send me the bird and the bill, please.»
—«Of course, I can't send you the bird without the bill.»

I'll buy this parrot, me quedo con este loro (al decidirse alguien por algo que compra en una tienda). || *I'll buy,* compraré.
bill significa «cuenta» (factura) y también «pico» (de ave), de ahí el chiste.

139

MR DYSON (to doctor on the phone): «My wife has caught a terrible cold and she has completely lost her voice too. Could you prescribe something to cure her cold?».

caught es el participio pasado de *catch* (coger, atrapar) y *lost,* participio pasado de *lose* (perder).
could you prescribe something to cure her cold? ¿podría usted recetar algo para curarle el resfriado? Literalmente: «curar su resfriado». || *could* se emplea en este caso con la idea de posibilidad.

140

BRICKLAYER (to helper below): «I'm sorry, but I couldn't prevent the brick from falling. It was quite accidental.»
HELPER: «Be careful up there, mate. You made me bite my tongue.»

I couldn't prevent the brick from falling, no pude evitar que se cayera el ladrillo. ‖ *couldn't* es la contracción de *could not* y en este caso se emplea como pasado de *can't.*
it was quite accidental, fue sin querer. Literalmente: «fue completamente accidental».
be careful up there, ten cuidado allá arriba.
made es el pasado de *make* (hacer).

141

An old man goes to the office where his grandson works and asks the porter:
—«Would you be so kind as to tell my grandson, Andrew Green, to come out for a moment?»
—«He's not in the office now», explains the porter. «He's gone to your funeral.»

would you be so kind as to tell my grandson...? ¿tendría usted la amabilidad de decir a mi nieto...? ‖ *would you be so kind as to* + infinitivo es la fórmula que se emplea para pedir algo cortésmente. Literalmente: «¿sería usted tan amable como para...?».
he's gone, se ha ido. ‖ *gone* es el participio pasado de *go* (ir, irse).

142

TENANT: «I'm very sorry, but I can't pay my rent this month.»
LANDLADY: «But you said that in March, in February and in January.»
TENANT: «Well, you can't say I didn't keep my word, can you?»

I can't pay my rent this month, no puedo pagar el alquiler este mes. || *rent* significa «renta» y también «alquiler» (de una vivienda). || *I can't* es la forma negativa y contracta de *I cannot,* no puedo.
you can't say I didn't keep my word, can you? no puede decir que no mantuve mi palabra, ¿verdad?

143

DOCTOR: «I'm afraid your disease is hereditary. It could possibly come from one of your great-great-grandparents. Well, that will be five pounds for the consultation.»
PATIENT: «Wait a minute! Send the bill to my great-great-grandfather, please!»

I'm afraid..., me temo que...
it could possibly come from..., posiblemente podría venir de...
great-great-grandparents, tatarabuelos.

144

Dick gets back home from school and says to his father:
—«Dad, we must love each other, mustn't we?»
—«Yes, Dick, that's true.»
—«Dad, there should be peace at home, shouldn't there?»
—«Certainly, Dick.»
—«Well, dad, in that case, you can have a look at my school marks.»

Dick gets back home from school, Dick vuelve a casa de la escuela.
there should be peace, debería haber paz.
you can have a look at my school marks, puedes echar un vistazo a mis notas de la escuela.

145

BOSS: «Well, Miss Williams, can you file?»
NEW SECRETARY (puzzled): «Well, yes, but why don't you engage a manicurist?»

can you file? ¿sabe usted archivar? También puede significar «¿sabe usted limar (las uñas)?», de ahí, el chiste.

146

MAN AT THE DOOR: «Excuse me, would you give me something to eat? I'm very hungry.»
MR DAVIS: «Wait a moment. I'll call my wife.»
MAN AT THE DOOR: «Thank you, sir, but I'm not a cannibal.»

would you give me something to eat? ¿me daría usted algo de comer? También: «¿querría usted darme...?». Nótese el uso de *something* en interrogativo, que normalmente se emplea en una petición.

147

At the recruiting office.
SERGEANT (to new recruit): «What's your full name?»
RECRUIT: «John Scott.»
SERGEANT: «You must always say "Sir" when you speak to a superior.»
RECRUIT (correcting): «Sir John Scott.»

what's your full name? ¿cuál es tu nombre completo?
you must always say..., debes decir siempre... || *must* en este caso se emplea con la idea de obligación.

148

LANDLADY (to Sammy, her tenants' son): «Is your dad or mum at home?»
SAMMY: «No, but will you come back on the 25th?»
LANDLADY: «Why on the 25th?»
SAMMY: «That's what I can't understand because we're moving on the 24th.»

is your dad or mum at home? ¿está en casa tu papá o tu mamá?
that's what I can't understand, eso es lo que no entiendo. Literalmente: «lo que no puedo entender.»
we're moving, nos mudamos.

149

EDWARD: «Dear, do you think you can live on my salary when we get married?»
RUTH: «Yes, but what will you live on?»

yes, but what will you live on?, sí, pero ¿de qué vivirás tú? Nótese la preposición al final de la oración. Esta forma se prefiere en la conversación normal a *«on what will you live?»*.

150

First Neighbour: «Can I borrow your hose, Mr Evans?»
Second Neighbour: «Oh, yes, of course, as long as you use it in my garden.»

as long as you use it in my garden, con tal de que la use en mi jardín.

151

Doctor: «Your husband must remain quiet for a fortnight at least. Here are some sleeping pills.»
Mrs Morris: «When must he take them?»
Doctor: «They aren't for him. They're for you.»

your husband must remain quiet, su marido debe permanecer tranquilo. || *must* se emplea en este caso con idea de necesidad.
for a fortnight at least, durante una quincena por lo menos.
sleeping pills, píldoras para dormir.

152

WIFE: «We must open a new bank account, dear.»
HUSBAND: «Why?»
WIFE: «Because there's no money left in the old one.»

we must open a new bank account, tenemos que abrir una nueva cuenta en el banco. || must se emplea con la idea de necesidad, en este caso.
there's no money left, no queda dinero.

153

DOCTOR: «Do you drink or smoke?»
PATIENT: «No, sir, never.»
DOCTOR: «Then, I'm sorry but I can't cure you.»
PATIENT: «Why?»
DOCTOR: «Because you have nothing to give up.»

I'm sorry, but I can't cure you, lo siento, pero no puedo curarle. || can't se emplea en este caso con la idea de imposibilidad.
you have nothing to give up, no tiene nada que dejar. || give up, dejar, abandonar (un vicio, una mala costumbre).

154

In the underground.
MAN: «Hey, can't you see you're putting your hand in my pocket?»
PICKPOCKET: «Excuse me, sir, but I used to have a coat exactly like that.»

hey! ¡oiga!
can't you see...? ¿no ve usted...? Literalmente: «¿no puede usted ver...?»
I used to have..., yo tenía... Literalmente: «yo solía tener...».

155

In a barber's shop.
MANICURIST (to playboy): «I can't go out with you. I'm married.»
PLAYBOY: «Ask your husband. He won't mind.»
MANICURIST: «You can ask him yourself. He's shaving you.»

he won't mind, a él no le importará. ‖ won't es la contracción de will not. ‖ mind, es «mente» y como verbo significa «importar».
you can ask him yourself, puede preguntarle usted mismo.

156

There was a knock on the door.
MR A: «Between!»
MR B: «Can I have a word with you, Mr A?»
MR A: «If.»

Un ejemplo del mal uso del diccionario: between significa «entre» (preposición) y la palabra if es la conjunción «si». Mr A. debería haber dicho, en el primer caso «come in!» y en el segundo «yes».

157

At an examination in a Military School.
SERGEANT: «How many jumps must a paratrooper make successfully to get his degree.»
PRIVATE: «All of them, sir.»

to get his degree, para graduarse. Literalmente: «para conseguir su graduación (grado)».
all of them, todos. Literalmente: «todos ellos».

158

WIFE: «We must dismiss our chauffeur.»
HUSBAND: «Why?»
WIFE: «He drives very carelessly. He almost killed me on two occasions yesterday.»
HUSBAND: «Give him another chance, dear.»

we must dismiss our chauffeur, tenemos que despedir a nuestro «chófer». ‖ Distíngase entre *driver*, conductor (de un vehículo) y *chauffeur*, «chófer» que lleva el coche de un señor.
he drives very carelessly, conduce con muy poco cuidado. Literalmente: «conduce muy descuidadamente». ‖ El sufijo *less* significa «sin»; *care*, «cuidado»; *careless*, «descuidado». ‖ *-ly* sirve para formar adverbios: *carelessly*, «descuidadamente».

159

HUSBAND: «Johnny has taken some money from my wallet.»
WIFE: «But you can't be sure Johnny took it. It may have been me.»
HUSBAND: «No, dear. I'm positive it wasn't you. There were eight pounds and now there are four.»

you can't be sure Johnny took it, no puedes estar seguro de que Johnny lo cogió. ‖ El verbo «coger» tiene tres formas: *take, took, taken*.
it may have been me, puedo haber sido yo. ‖ *may* se emplea con la idea de posibilidad, en este caso.

GRAMMAR AND HUMOUR

160

WILLY: «Look here, did you tell Joan I was stupid?»
ARTHUR: «Why should I tell her? Doesn't she know?»

look here! ¡oye! Literalmente: «¡mira aquí!».
why should I tell her? doesn't she know? ¿por qué habría de decírselo? ¿no lo sabe? Obsérvese que no se traduce normalmente el pronombre español «lo» en estos casos.

161

Wife to husband.
—«Tell your boss that if he can't raise your salary, he could give it to you twice a month.»

if he can't raise your salary, si no puede subirte el sueldo.
twice a month, dos veces al mes.

162

FATHER: «I can give my daughter a £3000 dowry. What can you give in return?»
PROSPECTIVE HUSBAND: «I can give you a receipt.»

what can you give in return? ¿qué puede usted dar a cambio?
receipt se pronuncia [ri'si:t]; la letra «p» es muda.

163

BASIL: «I'm so worried that I can't sleep at all.»
MARTIN: «What's the matter?»
BASIL: «I haven't got enough money to pay my debts.»
MARTIN: «I think I can solve your problem.»
BASIL: «Really? Can you lend me some money?»
MARTIN: «No, but I know of a very good cure for insomnia.»

at all, en absoluto.
what's the matter? ¿qué ocurre?
enough money, bastante dinero.
debts se pronuncia [dets]; la letra «b» es muda.
can you lend me some money? ¿puede prestarme (algo de) dinero?

164

WIFE: «Bruce, don't go to sleep yet. I'm talking to you.»
HUSBAND: «I'm sorry, darling. I must sleep some time.»

don't go to sleep yet, no te duermas aún. || Distíngase entre *to go to sleep,* quedarse dormido y *to go to bed,* irse a dormir.
I must sleep some time, debo dormir algo. || *some time,* algún tiempo. || *must* se emplea aquí con el sentido de necesidad.

165

In the country.
POSTMAN (to farmer): «Now I've got to walk five miles to Mr Wilson's farm to deliver this parcel.»
FARMER: «Why take such trouble? It would be easier to send it by post.»

I've got to walk five miles to Mr Wilson's farm, tengo que andar cinco millas hasta la granja de Mr Wilson.
why take such trouble? ¿por qué molestarse? Literalmente: «¿por qué tomar tal molestia?»
by post, por correo.

166

MEMBER OF THE NOUVEAU RICHE: «Come round for dinner tomorrow.»
FRIEND: «I'm sorry, but I can't. I'm going to see Hamlet tomorrow.»
MEMBER OF THE NOUVEAU RICHE: «Never mind, bring him with you. There's enough food for both of you.»

come round for dinner tomorrow, ven a cenar mañana.
never mind, no importa.
for both of you, para los dos (para vosotros dos). ‖ *both* = ambos.

167

At a party.
JEAN: «Jack, why are you sitting at the piano? You can't play a single note.»
JACK: «Nor can anybody else while I'm sitting here.»

you can't play a single note, no sabes (no puedes) tocar ni una nota.
nor can anybody else, ni tampoco puede nadie más. || Nótense los dos significados del verbo *can* en este chiste: «saber» y «poder».

168

Just after the wedding.
BRIDEGROOM: «Can you cook, dear?»
BRIDE: «Of course, I can. Mother taught me the day before yesterday.»

can you cook? ¿sabes guisar?
of course, I can, pues claro que sé. || En estos dos casos *can* se traduce por «saber».
taught es el pasado y participio pasado de *teach* (enseñar).
the day before yesterday, anteayer.

169

PEPE: «You say that you're learning English at a correspondence school and that sometimes you play truant. How can you do that?»
PACO: «Well, once or twice a month I send them an empty envelope.»

to play truant, hacer novillos.
once or twice a month, una o dos veces al mes.

170

DOCTOR: «Now, Mrs Hinkley, put this thermometer in your mouth and keep your lips closed for a moment.»
MR HINKLEY: «Oh, what a wonderful instrument! Where can I get one, doctor?»

keep your lips closed for a moment, mantenga los labios cerrados un momento.
where can I get one? ¿dónde puedo conseguir uno?

171

DOCTOR: «What's the matter with you?»
PATIENT: «In the morning I have such a terrible pain that I can't get to sleep.»
DOCTOR: «And where do you feel this pain?»
PATIENT: «In the office.»

what's the matter with you? ¿qué le pasa a usted?
I can't get to sleep, no puedo dormirme.

172

In a flower shop.
MAN: «I'd like some potted roses.»
FLORIST: «I'm sorry. We're out of roses just now, but we've got some very nice carnations.»
MAN: «Oh, no, I promised my wife I'd water her roses while she was away and she's coming back home today.»

in a flower shop, en una floristería.
I'd like some potted roses, quiero un tiesto con rosas. Literalmente: «me gusta-

rían algunas rosas en tiesto». || *I'd like* es una fórmula muy corriente que se usa para pedir algo en una tienda.

I promised my wife I'd water her roses, prometí a mi mujer que le regaría las rosas (regaría sus rosas). || *I'd water* es la contracción de *I would water*.

173

At a party.
FIRST GUEST (with a long beard): «Don't you remember me? I'm Jack Harris. We were both in the same class at the Arundel School some thirty years ago.»
SECOND GUEST (trying to remember): «No, you can't have been. Nobody in my class had a beard.»

some thirty years ago, hace unos treinta años.
we were both, los dos estuvimos.
you can't have been, usted no puede haber sido.

174

BARBARA: «Aunt, last night I dreamt you had given me a five-pound note.»
AUNT: «OK, Barbara, as you're a good girl, you can keep it.»

last night I dreamt you had given me a five-pound note, anoche soñé que me habías dado un billete de cinco libras. || *dreamt* es el pasado y participio pasado de *dream* (soñar). || *given* es el participio pasado de *give* (dar).
you can keep it, puedes quedarte con ello.

175

PATIENT: «Well, doctor, I've come to see you because I have the Monday morning feeling.»
DOCTOR: «Well, so have most people. It's quite common. So you needn't worry.»
PATIENT: «Yes, doctor, but I have it every day.»

I have the Monday morning feeling, tengo la sensación del lunes por la mañana.
so have most people, también lo tiene la mayoría de la gente.
you needn't worry, no tiene usted por qué preocuparse.

IX PRONOMBRES RELATIVOS
(RELATIVE PRONOUNS)

176

In the Far West, the sheriff looks sternly at Bill, who has broken the law, and says:
—«Either ten days in jail or a hundred dollars.»
Bill, without hesitating, exclaims:
—«I'll take the hundred dollars!»

the sheriff looks sternly at Bill, who has broken the law, el «sheriff» mira con cara de pocos amigos a Bill, que ha quebrantado la ley. ‖ *who* es pronombre relativo que se usa después de persona. En este caso le precede una coma (,) ya que se trata de una oración de tipo *non-defining.*
either ten days in jail or a hundred dollars, (o) diez días de cárcel o cien dólares. ‖ *either... or* significa «o... o».

177

TEACHER (to Bob, who is talking to his companion in class):
«Bob, I wish you would pay a little attention.»
BOB: «I'm paying as little attention as I can, sir.»

Bob, who is talking to his companion in class, Bob, que está hablando con su compañero de clase. Véase 176.
I wish you would pay a little attention, a ver si pones un poco de atención. Literalmente: «deseo (sería de desear) que pongas un poco de atención». ‖ *to pay attention,* poner atención.

178

Mrs Williams is giving orders to Molly, the new maid she has just engaged.
MRS WILLIAMS: «We always have breakfast at half-past eight.»
MOLLY: «Well, ma'am, if I'm not up on time, don't wait for me. I'll have breakfast later on.»

Mrs Williams is giving orders to Molly, the new maid she has just engaged,
  Mrs Williams está dando instrucciones a Molly, la nueva criada que acaba de contratar. Hay que observar la omisión del pronombre relativo: *the new maid (who/that) she has just engaged.* Es muy corriente omitir el pronombre relativo cuando éste hace de objeto directo.
on time, a tiempo.
later on, más tarde.

179

The announcer of a radio programme asked a housewife who had just won a £100 prize for having answered three questions right:
—«And now, what are you going to do with the money you've won?»
—«Count it», answered the housewife quickly.

the announcer of a radio programme asked a housewife who had just won a £ 100 prize, el locutor de un programa de radio preguntó a un ama de casa que acababa de ganar un premio de 100 libras. || *who* no va precedido de coma (,) porque se trata de una oración de tipo *defining*.

180

MICK: «I can see you are the perfect married man. No buttons off your shirt now.»
GORDON: «Well, the first thing my wife taught me was how to sew them on.»

no buttons off your shirt now, ahora no te faltan botones en la camisa. Literalmente: «ningún botón fuera de tu camisa ahora». Se sobreentiende: *there are no buttons...*
the first thing my wife taught me, la primera cosa que mi mujer me enseñó. Está omitido el pronombre relativo: *the first thing (that) my wife... || taught* es el pasado del verbo *teach* (enseñar).

181

GRANNY: «I'll buy you a parrot provided you don't teach him to swear.»
ALEC: «All right, granny, I'll teach him the words he mustn't say.»

provided you don't teach him to swear, con tal de que no le enseñes a decir palabrotas.
I'll teach him the words he mustn't say, le enseñaré las palabras que no debe decir. El pronombre relativo *(that/which)* está omitido detrás de *words*. || El negativo de un verbo anómalo se forma colocando simplemente *not* detrás: *must not;* en forma contracta: *mustn't*.

182

WILLY: «Mum, does a bowl of soup do any harm?»
MUM: «Oh, no, dear, not at all. Why do you ask?»
WILLY: «Because I've just spilt a bowl of soup on the fur coat daddy gave you for your birthday.»

I've just spilt a bowl of soup on the fur coat daddy gave you for your birthday, acabo de verter un plato de sopa en el abrigo de pieles que papa te regaló por tu cumpleaños. El pronombre relativo *(that/which)* está omitido detrás de la palabra *coat*. ‖ *spilt* es el pasado y participio pasado del verbo *spill* (verter, derramar). ‖ *gave* es el pasado del verbo *(give)* dar, regalar.

183

MR LYONS: «I really admire my dentist.»
FRIEND: «Your dentist? Why?»
MR LYONS: «Well, he's the only fellow who can make my wife keep her mouth shut for half an hour.»

he's the only fellow who can make my wife keep her mouth shut, él es el único individuo que puede hacer que mi mujer tenga la boca cerrada. ‖ *who* en este caso no se omite porque hace oficio de sujeto.

184

There's a knock at the door.
HOTEL BOY: «Are you the gentleman who wanted to get up early to catch the seven o'clock train?»
GUEST: «Yes.»
HOTEL BOY: «Well, sir, you can go back to sleep again, because you've just missed it.»

are you the gentleman who wanted to get up early...? ¿es usted el señor que quería levantarse temprano...? El pronombre relativo *who* está en el mismo caso que en 183.
you've just missed it, lo acaba usted de perder.

185

POLICEMAN (on the phone): «Is that Mr Jackson? We've just caught the thief who stole your car.»
MR JACKSON: «Don't let him go.»
POLICEMAN: «No, we won't, but why?»
MR JACKSON: «Because I want to ask him how he got it to start.»

we've just caught the thief who stole your car, acabamos de atrapar al ladrón que robó su coche. El caso del pronombre relativo *who* es el mismo que en 183 y 184. ‖ *caught* es el pasado y participio pasado del verbo *catch* (atrapar). ‖ *stole* es el pasado del verbo *steal* (robar).

186

At a restaurant.
OWNER (to customer): «Did the waiter you are complaining about have a big moustache?»
CUSTOMER: «Well, he didn't when he took my order.»

did the waiter you are complaining about have a big moustache? ¿tenía un bigote grande el camarero de quien se queja usted? En inglés corriente, cuando un pronombre relativo va precedido de preposición, dicho pronombre se omite y la preposición pasa después del verbo. La frase completa sería: *did the waiter about whom you are complaining have a big moustache?*

187

At court.
JUDGE: «Why did you break into the same department store four nights running?»
THIEF: «Well, sir, the first night I took a blouse for my wife and I had to change it three times till I found one that suited her.»

why did you break into the same department store four nights running? ¿por qué entró usted en el mismo almacén cuatro noches consecutivas? ‖ *break into* = entrar por la fuerza (en un lugar).
I took a blouse for my wife, cogí una blusa para mi mujer. ‖ *took* es el pasado de *take* (tomar, coger).
till I found one that suited her, hasta que encontré una que le sentaba bien. El pronombre relativo *that* no está omitido porque hace oficio de sujeto. ‖ *found* es el pasado y participio pasado de *find* (encontrar).

188

BOSS: «That's a very shabby suit you're wearing, Murray.»
CLERK: «Yes, I know. I bought it the last time I got a rise.»

that's a very shabby suit you're wearing, lleva usted un traje muy raído. El pronombre relativo está omitido detrás de la palabra *suit*. Literalmente: «ese es un traje muy raído (un muy raído traje) (el) que usted lleva». || Nótese la forma progresiva: *you're wearing*, ya que se trata de una acción que ocurre en el momento en que habla el personaje.
bought es el pasado y participio pasado de *buy* (comprar).

189

DOOR-TO-DOOR SALESMAN (to housewife): «I would like to show you the new vacuum cleaner that your next door neighbour says you can't afford.»

door-to-door salesman, vendedor que va de puerta en puerta.
that, el pronombre relativo que aparece detrás de *vacuum cleaner* (aspiradora), podrá omitirse ya que hace de objeto directo.
your next door neighbour, su vecino de al lado.
you can't afford, usted no puede permitirse el lujo (de tener o de comprar).

190

Mrs Briggs, who is very fat, is eating a big piece of cake when her neighbour drops in:
NEIGHBOUR: «I thought you were on a diet.»
MRS BRIGGS: «I am. First I have my diet and then I eat my lunch.»

who, el pronombre relativo detrás de Mrs Briggs, va precedido de coma (,) por la misma razón que se expone en 176.
when her neighbour drops in, cuando su vecina la visita. || *drop in* = pasar de visita.
I thought you were on a diet, creía que estabas a dieta. || *to be on a diet* = estar a dieta. || *thought* es el pasado y participio pasado de *think* (creer, pensar).

191

Overheard in a bus.
—«I consider a very poor man the one who forgets his wife's birthday.»
—«Well, I consider a much poorer man the one who remembers it.»

the one who forgets his wife's birthday, el que olvida el cumpleaños de su mujer. Nótese *the one who,* el que, la que.

192

At a party, a waiter tripped over a chair and the four glasses he was carrying on a tray fell on top of a gentleman who was sitting on a sofa. The waiter apologized and the gentleman said:
—«Thank goodness they were dry martinis!»

and the four glasses he was carrying on a tray, y los cuatro vasos que llevaba en una bandeja. El pronombre relativo está omitido detrás de *glasses,* ya que hace oficio de objeto directo.
on top of, sobre, encima.
a gentleman who was sitting, un señor que estaba sentado. El pronombre relativo *who* no se puede omitir porque hace oficio de sujeto.
thank goodness! ¡gracias a Dios!

193

A VIP attending a dinner was surprised to see that the girl who took the coats at the door gave no tickets in return.
—«She has a wonderful memory», somebody explained.
As the VIP was leaving, the girl handed him his coat.
—«How do you know this one is mine?», he asked her.
—«I don't know, sir», replied the girl.
—«Then why are you giving it to me?»
—«Because you gave it to me first.»

a VIP, un personaje importante. ‖ VIP (Very Important Person).
the girl who took the coats at the door, la chica que cogía los abrigos a la puerta. El caso de *who* es el mismo que el que se comenta en 192.
in return, a cambio.
took es el pasado de *take* (tomar, coger) y *gave* es el pasado de *give* (dar).

194

MAN: «Are you the boy who rescued my son from the river?»
BOY: «Yes, I am.»
MAN: «Well, where's the toy car I bought him?»

are you the boy who rescued...? ¿eres el muchacho que rescató...? El caso de *who* es el mismo que el que se comenta en 192.
where's the toy car I bought him? ¿dónde está el cochecito que le compré? Está omitido el pronombre relativo detrás de *toy car*, que significa «cochecito de juguete».

195

KAREN: «Why doesn't your uncle work?»
KIM: «Because he's very superstitious.»
KAREN: «So what?»
KIM: «He refuses to work any week that has a Friday in it.»

so what? ¿y qué?
he refuses to work any week that has a Friday in it, se niega trabajar cualquier semana que tenga viernes. ‖ *any* en oración afirmativa significa «cualquier». ‖ El pronombre relativo *that* que va detrás de *week* no se omite porque hace de sujeto. ‖ *Friday* es el día fatídico en el mundo de habla inglesa. ‖ Los días de la semana se escriben en inglés con mayúscula.

196

Once a housewife was cleaning her upstairs windows when she accidentally fell out and landed in a dust-bin in the street. A foreigner who happened to pass by, saw the woman in the dust-bin and said:
—«The English are very wasteful. I would have thought that this woman would be useful for a few more years.»

when she accidentally fell out, cuando ella casualmente se cayó (hacia afuera). ‖ *fell* es el pasado de *fall* (caer).

a foreigner who happened to pass by, un extranjero que pasaba por allí de casualidad. ‖ *happen* = ocurrir. Nótese esta otra acepción de *happen: I happened to meet him,* me encontré con él por casualidad. El comentario sobre el pronombre relativo *who* es el mismo que en la nota 192.

I would have thought, yo habría pensado. ‖ *thought* es el pasado y participio pasado de *think* (pensar).

197

HORACE: «Why did you give the waiter two pounds? Isn't it too much for a tip?»
BERNARD: «Yes, but look at the new hat he's just given me.»

look at the new hat he's just given me, mira el sombrero nuevo que me acaba de dar. El pronombre relativo está omitido detrás de *hat.* || *he's just* = *he has just.* || *given* es el participio pasado de *give* (dar).

198

HUGH: «Yesterday I met a boy exactly like you.»
OLIVER: «I hope you didn't pay him back the ten pounds I lent you a year ago.»

met es el pasado y participio pasado de *meet* encontrar (a alguien).
the ten pounds I lent you, las diez libras que te presté. El pronombre relativo está omitido detrás de *pounds.* || *lent* es el pasado y participio pasado de *lend* (prestar).

199

One morning a tourist brushed his teeth in the lavatory of a railway carriage. When he returned to his seat he realized that he had left his tooth-brush on the wash-basin, so he went back to fetch it. The door was locked. He knocked and a man who was brushing his teeth opened the door and said:
—«What's the matter?»
—«Are you brushing your teeth with my tooth-brush?», asked the tourist.
—«Your tooth-brush?», the man replied. «I thought it belonged to the Railway Company.»

... brushed his teeth, ... se lavaba los dientes. || *brush* = cepillar.
railway carriage, vagón de tren.
he realized that he had left his tooth-brush, se dio cuenta de que había dejado el (su) cepillo de dientes. La palabra *that* detrás de *realized* es una conjunción, ya que va después de un verbo. || *left* es el pasado y participio pasado de *leave* (dejar).
a man who was brushing his teeth, un hombre que se estraba lavando los dientes. El pronombre relativo *who* hace de sujeto. Véase 192.

200

Two friends, who hadn't seen each other for a long time, met in the street.
FIRST FRIEND: «How's life, Dan? I can see that you are married.»
SECOND FRIEND: «Yes. How did you guess it?»
FIRST FRIEND: «Before, your clothes always used to look wrinkled and now you look very smart.»
SECOND FRIEND: «Well, that's because my wife made me iron this suit today.»

two friends, who hadn't seen each other for a long time, dos amigos, que no se habían visto durante mucho tiempo. *Who* con coma (,) delante se comenta en 176. || *each other* es pronombre recíproco.

X ORACIONES CONDICIONALES *(CONDITIONAL SENTENCES)*

201

In a religion class.
TEACHER: «Do you know how many Commandments there are?»
BOY: «Yes, sir. There are ten.»
TEACHER: «All right, and now tell me, if you broke one of them, what would happen?»
BOY: «Then there would be only nine, sir.»

if you broke one of them, what would happen? si quebrantaras (rompieras) uno de ellos, ¿qué ocurriría? En una oración condicional, de las llamadas en inglés *Hypothetical Conditions,* la oración subordinada (que comienza por *if*) lleva el verbo en pasado, y la oración principal se forma con *would* + infinitivo (sin *to*). ‖ *if you broke* puede también traducirse por: «si se quebrantara (rompiera)», en sentido impersonal. ‖ *broke* es el pasado del verbo *break* (romper).

202

MAN: «What would happen if somebody came to your restaurant, had lunch and didn't pay?»
OWNER: «I'd kick him out of the restaurant.»
MAN: «Well, that's not too bad. Bring me a bowl of onion soup and a pork chop.»

What would happen...? ¿qué ocurriría...?
if somebody came to your restaurant, si alguien viniera a su restaurante. Véase 201.
I'd kick him out of the restaurant, le echaría del restaurante de una patada. ‖
  I'd es la contracción de *I would*.

203

FIRST NEIGHBOUR: «I hear you have Mr Anderson's hammer.»
SECOND NEIGHBOUR: «Yes, I have. So what?»
FIRST NEIGHBOUR: «Well, if you let me use it, I'll let you have his tongs.»

if you let me use it, I'll let you have his tongs, si me deja usarlo, yo le dejaré sus tenazas. En una condicional, de las llamadas en inglés *Open Conditions*, la oración subordinada (que empieza por *if*) lleva el verbo en presente, y la oración principal se construye en futuro.

204

MRS DAWSON: «A month ago my husband went to the supermarket to buy a tin of marmalade and he never returned. What would you do in my place?»
MRS ADAMS: «If I were in your place, I'd go to the supermarket and buy another tin of marmalade.»

what would you do in my place? ¿qué haría usted en mi lugar? ‖ *would* sirve para formar el potencial. Nótese: *I do,* yo hago; *I would do,* yo haría.
if I were in your place, I'd go to the supermarket, si yo estuviera en su lugar, iría al supermercado. Véase 201. ‖ *I'd go* = *I would go.* ‖ Nótese *were* con la primera persona del singular: *I,* en este tipo de oración.
marmalade = mermelada de naranja. Cualquier otra clase de mermelada se denomina en inglés *jam*.

205

Mrs Porter: «I'm going shopping, Betty. Bath the baby. Don't forget to use the thermometer to check the temperature of the water.»
Au-pair Girl: «There's no need to use a thermometer, madam.»
Mrs Porter: «Then, how do you know?»
Au-pair Girl: «It's very easy. If the baby turns blue, the water is too cold. If he turns red, the water is too hot.»

if the baby turns blue, the water is too cold, si el niño se vuelve azul, el agua está demasiado fría. En esta condición: *Open Condition,* la oración subordinada lleva el verbo en presente, así como la oración principal.

206

In the cinema.
Attendant (to a young couple with their baby): «If the baby begins to cry, you will have to take your money back and leave the cinema.»
Ten minutes after the beginning of the film:
Wife: «It's a very boring film, isn't it?»
Husband: «Yes, it is. Let's pinch Timmy and get our money back.»

if the baby begins to cry, you will have to take your money back and leave the cinema, si el niño empieza a llorar, tendrán que recobrar su dinero (les devolverán el dinero) y se irán del cine (abandonarán el cine). Véase 203.

let's pinch Timmy and get our money back, pellizquemos a Tommy y que nos devuelvan el dinero. Literalmente: «recobremos nuestro dinero».

207

DOUGLAS: «Some people say that it's bad luck if a black cat crosses your path. Do you think it's true?»
JOAN: «Well, it all depends on whether you consider yourself a mouse or a person.»

do you think it's true? ¿crees que es verdad? ǁ *true* = verdadero.

it all depends on whether you consider yourself a mouse or a person, todo depende de si te consideras un ratón o una persona. ǁ *yourself* es pronombre reflexivo.

Para la construcción de la oración condicional, véase 205.

208

A young man bought an engagement ring for his fiancée and said to the jeweller:
—«I'd like to have the words "From Larry to Alison" engraved on the ring.»
—«If I were you», the jeweller said, «I'd only have: "From Larry".»

engagement ring = sortija de compromiso.

I'd like to have the words «From Larry to Alison» engraved on the ring, me gustaría que me grabaran en la sortija las palabras «De Larry a Alison». Literalmente: «me gustaría tener las palabras From L. to A. grabadas en la sortija».

Para la construcción de la oración condicional, véase 201.

209

AUNT: «If you wash your hands, I'll give you a sweet. If you wash your face as well, I'll give you three sweets. If you wash your neck, I'll give you five sweets.»
PHILIP: «How many sweets will you give me if I have a shower?»

as well, también.
if I have a shower, si me doy una ducha. ‖ *to have a shower* = ducharse, darse una ducha.
Para la construcción de las oraciones condicionales, véase 203.

210

In class.
TEACHER: «If your father owed 5 pounds to the baker, 6 pounds to the fishmonger and 10 pounds to the grocer, how much would he have to pay in all?»
BOY: «Nothing, because we'd move to another neighbourhood.»

how much would he have to pay in all? ¿cuánto tendría que pagar en total?
we'd move to another neighbourhood, nos mudaríamos a otra vecindad.
Para la construcción de la oración condicional, véase 201.

211

BRUCE: «Why don't you believe in statistics?»
JAMES: «Well, you see, if you eat one chicken and I don't eat anything, according to statistics, we've both eaten half a chicken.»

if you eat one chicken and I don't eat anything..., si tú te comes un pollo y yo no como nada... (oraciones subordinadas en presente).
we've both eaten half a chicken, los dos hemos comido medio pollo (oración principal en *present perfect*).

212

On the first day at school.
TEACHER: «If anyone has to go to the lavatory he must hold up two fingers.»
PUPIL (at the back of the class): «Sir, does that really help?»

if anyone has to go to the lavatory, he must hold up two fingers, si alguien tiene que ir al lavabo, debe levantar dos dedos. La oración subordinada, en presente, y la principal, en presente también, con un verbo anómalo: *must*.

213

PATIENT: «How much do you charge for taking a tooth out?»
DENTIST: «Five pounds.»
PATIENT: «Five pounds for taking a tooth out! That's what I call earning money easily and quickly. It's only a question of five minutes!»
DENTIST: «Well, if you like, I can take your tooth out very slowly.»

how much do you charge for taking a tooth out? ¿cuánto cobra por sacar un diente? Obsérvese *for* + *gerund* = por + infinitivo, en español.
Para la construcción de la oración condicional, véase 212.

214

SCHOOL INSPECTOR (to pupil): «Who wrote Hamlet?»
PUPIL: «I didn't, sir.»
SCHOOL INSPECTOR (to teacher): «What have you got to say about this boy?»
TEACHER: «I can assure you Ben is a truthful boy. If he says he didn't do it, you must believe him.»

I can assure you Ben is a truthful boy, puedo asegurarle que B. es un chico que dice la verdad. ‖ *truthful,* veraz, verídico, verdadero: *truth* = verdad; *truthful* = lleno de verdad.
Para la construcción de la oración condicional, véase 212.

XI · GERUNDIO *(GERUND)*

215

HARRY: «I hear your wife has to support you by going out charring.»
TIM: «Oh, yes. She's too ignorant to get a better job.»

your wife has to support you by going out charring, tu mujer tiene que mantenerte trabajando de asistenta. Nótese la forma *gerund* después de una preposición: *by going...* En este caso se traduce por gerundio en español.

216

MIKE: «The other day I decided to save 30p, so instead of catching the bus I ran home after it.»
PETER: «Well, next time run home after a taxi, and you'll save 3 pounds.»

instead of catching the bus, I ran after it, en vez de tomar el autobús, corrí tras él. El *gerund* detrás de una preposición: *instead of catching,* se traduce en este caso por un infinitivo en español.

217

During a cookery lesson.
MONITOR: «How can you keep sardines from smelling?»
MRS WEST (after thinking for a minute): «By cutting off their noses!»

how can you keep sardines from smelling?, ¿cómo pueden ustedes evitar que huelan las sardinas? En este caso, el *gerund*, después de preposición: *from smelling*, se traduce en español por una oración sustantiva: «que huelan las sardinas» o «que las sardinas huelan». El chiste reside en los dos sentidos del verbo *smell* = oler: a) despedir olor (intransitivo); b) recibir los olores (transitivo).

218

INTERVIEWER (to ninety-year-old man): «I hope to have the pleasure of interviewing you again when you're hundred years old.»
OLD MAN: «Why not? You look quite healthy to me.»

the pleasure of interviewing you again, el placer de entrevistarle a usted otra vez. El *gerund* después de preposición: *of interviewing*, se traduce en español por infinitivo, en este caso.

219

DOCTOR: «Well, well! So after treating you for jaundice for three years, you say now that you are Chinese!»

after treating you for jaundice, después de tratarle a usted de ictericia. La forma *gerund,* en este caso, se traduce al español por un infinitivo.

220

TRAFFIC POLICEMAN: «Didn't you hear my whistle, madam?»
WOMAN DRIVER: «Yes, but I don't like flirting while I'm driving.»

I don't like flirting while I'm driving, no me gusta coquetear mientras conduzco. Nótese el *gerund* detrás del verbo *like.*
Cuando la forma *ing* del verbo va después del verbo *to be,* se denomina *present participle,* y no *gerund,* tal es el caso de *driving.*

221

A man went into a pub, sat down and asked for a glass of water and quietly drank it. As he was going out, the waiter looked at him sternly:
—«Why are you looking at me like that?» asked the man.
—«Because you have the cheek to come in here, sit down, drink a glass of water and then walk out.»
—«After drinking a glass of water, do you expect me to stagger out?»

as he was going out, cuando salía.
you have the cheek, tiene usted la cara dura.
after drinking a glass of water, do you expect me to stagger out?, después de beberme un vaso de agua, ¿espera usted que salga tambaleándome? Nótese el *gerund* después de preposición: *after drinking.*
Véase 220 (última nota), por lo que respecta a *looking.*

222

MR HUDSON: «I don't like living in this house.»
MR WARD: «Why not?»
MR HUDSON: «Because the next-door neighbour is an undertaker.»
MR WARD: «So what?»
MR HUDSON: «Well, when I meet him in the lift, he says "Good mourning" to me in a gloomy way.»

I don't like living in this house, no me gusta vivir en esta casa. || Véase 220.
so what? ¿y qué?
mourning, luto y *morning*, mañana se pronuncian igual, de ahí el chiste.

223

An old man said to the telephone operator after using the phone.
—«You've been very kind to me, Miss. So I'm going to put a penny in the slot for your trouble.»

after using the phone, después de usar el teléfono. || Véase 221.
for your trouble, por su molestia (por la molestia que se ha tomado).
I'm going to put a penny, voy a poner un penique. || Véase 224 (1.ª nota).

224

A man is applying for a post in a factory.
SECRETARY (filling out a form): «How long married?»
MAN (without hesitating): «Twenty-four hours a day.»

a man is applying for a post in a factory, un hombre está solicitando (solicita) un puesto en una fábrica. || *applying* no es *gerund*, ya que va detrás del verbo *to be*, sino *present participle*.
without hesitating, sin vacilar. Nótese el *gerund* detrás de preposición *(without)*.

225

A kind gentleman offered to help a lady change a wheel of her car. When he finished changing it and was trying to let the jack down, the lady exclaimed:
—«Please be careful. My husband is sleeping in the back.»

when he finished changing it, cuando terminó de cambiarla. Hay que notar el uso del *gerund* detrás del verbo *finished.* || Véase 220.
and was trying to let the jack down, y estaba tratando de bajar el gato. || Véase 224 (1.ª nota).
my husband is sleeping, mi marido está durmiendo. || Véase 224 (1.ª nota).

226

Once an air-liner was flying over the Atlantic. A naughty boy, about then years old, was running wild up and down the corridor playing at being a cowboy, while the airhostess tried in vain to stop him. The boy was shouting at the top of his voice when a lady said to him:
—«Come on, little boy, why don't you go out to play?»

an air-liner was flying, un avión de pasajeros estaba volando (volaba). || Véase 224 (1.ª nota).
... was running wild up and down the corridor, estaba corriendo (corría) sin control por el pasillo. || *up and down* = arriba y abajo. || Véase 224 (1.ª nota).
playing at being a cowboy, jugando a los vaqueros. Literalmente: «jugando a ser un vaquero». || *at being,* a ser. Preposición + *gerund.*
the boy was shouting, el chico estaba gritando (gritaba). || Véase 224 (1.ª nota).

227

A workman was making holes for planting trees. A curious old man went up to him and asked:
—«What are you digging for?»
—«I'm digging for money.»
—«For money?» exclaimed the astonished old man. «Tell me, when do you expect to get it?»
—«On payday», said the man and went on digging.

... was making holes, ... estaba haciendo (hacía) agujeros. ‖ Véase 224 (1.ª nota).
what are you digging for?, ¿para qué está usted cavando? ‖ Véase 224 (1.ª nota).
I'm digging, estoy cavando. ‖Véase 224 (1.ª nota).
and went on digging, y siguió cavando. Hay que notar el uso del *gerund* después de la partícula *on*.

228

TEACHER: «Tell me, Johnny, which is the best time to pick pears, spring, summer, autumn or winter?»
JOHNNY (without hesitating): «The best time to pick pears is when the farmer is not at home and there's no dog on the farm.»

which is the best time to pick pears?, ¿cuál es la mejor época para coger peras?
without hesitating, sin vacilar. ‖ Véase 224.

229

Mrs Field was sitting by her little son's bed telling him a story, when the child said:
—«Mummy, please stop talking about Cinderella and let me go to sleep.»

Mrs Field was sitting by her little son's bed, telling him a story, Mrs F. estaba sentada al lado de la cama de su niño contándole un cuento. ‖ Véase 224 (1.ª nota).
stop talking about Cinderella, deja de hablar de la Cenicienta. ‖ Después del verbo *stop* sigue *gerund.*

230

TIM: «The other day I read an article in a magazine about the harmful effects of alcohol. It said drinking whisky was very bad for the health.»
CHARLES: «Did it make you decide to give up drinking?»
TIM: «No, it made me decide to give up reading.»

it said drinking whisky was very bad for the health, decía que beber whisky era muy malo para la salud. || En este caso el *gerund* hace oficio de sujeto de la oración. En español: «el beber whisky...».

give up drinking, dejar de beber; *give up reading,* dejar de leer. || *give up* = abandonar (una costumbre). En ambos casos aparece *gerund* después de la partícula *up.*

231

ANDY: «Why are you so fat?»
FAT MAN: «Because I don't like arguing.»
ANDY: «Bah, I'm sure that isn't the reason.»
FAT MAN: «Well, if you say so, perhaps you're right.»

because I don't like arguing, porque no me gusta discutir. || Véase 220.
if you say so, si usted lo dice.
perhaps you're right, quizá tenga usted razón. || *to be right,* tener razón.

232

Albert is telling Fred how optimistic people get on very well in life:
—«My friend Kenneth is so optimistic that the other day, without having a penny in his pocket, he went into a restaurant and asked for a dozen oysters in the hope of paying the bill with the pearl he was sure to find inside one of them.»

Albert is telling Fred, A. le cuenta a F. || *telling* es un *present participle* porque va precedido del verbo *to be.*
how optimistic people get on very well in life, cómo a la gente optimista le va bien en la vida.
without having a penny in his pocket, sin tener un penique en el bolsillo. || Véase 228.
... went into a restaurant, ... entró en un restaurante. || *went* es el pasado del verbo *to go* (ir).
in the hope of paying, con la esperanza de pagar. || *paying* es un *gerund* por ir después de *of.*
he was sure to find, estaba seguro de encontrar.

233

At a history examination.
EXAMINER: «Mention an important event in 1564.»
EXAMINEE (after thinking for a long time): «Shakespeare was born.»
EXAMINER: «Very well, and in 1574?»
EXAMINEE: «Let me think... ah, yes. I know. Shakespeare's tenth birthday!»

after thinking for a long time, después de pensar un buen rato. Literalmente: «un largo tiempo». ‖ Véase 221.

234

Mary and Jack have just seen Hamlet.
JACK: «Why did you look so embarrassed after the play?»
MARY: «Because you began shouting, author, author!»

seen es el participio pasado de see (ver).
you began shouting, tú empezaste a gritar. ‖ Después del verbo begin puede usarse el gerund o el infinitivo sin to, así se puede decir también: you began to shout.

235

After the party.
MRS WHEELER: «Didn't you notice Mr Andrews? He kept on yawning when I was talking.»
MR WHEELER: «He wasn't yawning, dear. He was only trying to say something.»

he kept on yawning, no dejaba de bostezar. ‖ Después de keep on = no dejar de (hacer algo), se usa el gerund.
he was only trying to say, sólo trataba de decir. Literalmente: «sólo estaba tratando de decir». ‖ Véase 232 (1.ª nota).

236

SAM: «Daddy, I don't want to go to New Zealand! It's too far away!»
DADDY: «Shut up, Sam, and carry on swimming!»

shup up! ¡cállate!
carry on swimming, sigue nadando. ‖ Después de *carry on* sigue el *gerund.*

237

WOMAN (to photographer): «The photo you took of my wedding group is horrible. Look at my husband. He looks like a frog.»
PHOTOGRAPHER: «I think it's too late now. You should have noticed that before marrying him, ma'am.»

took es el pasado de *take* (tomar).
he looks like a frog, parece una rana.
before marrying him, ma'am, antes de casarse con él, señora. ‖ *marrying* es un gerund por ir después de *before.* ‖ *ma'am = madam.*

XII VOZ PASIVA
(PASSIVE VOICE)

238

MAN: «There used to be a sign here which read THIEVES WILL BE PROSECUTED, didn't there?»
SHOP OWNER: «Oh, yes, but it was stolen a month ago.»

thieves will be prosecuted, los ladrones serán procesados.
it was stolen a month ago, lo robaron hace un mes. Literalmente: «fue robado hace un mes». ‖ *stolen* es el participio pasado de *steal* (robar).
El verbo *read* [ri:d], leer, hace el pasado y el participio pasado de la misma manera: *read*, pero se pronuncia [red].

239

WIFE: «We'll have to go to a restaurant for dinner. The electricity was cut off and I couldn't prepare any food.»
HUSBAND: «But we cook by gas.»
WIFE: «Yes, but the tin opener is electric.»

the electricity was cut off, han cortado la luz (electricidad). Literalmente: «la electricidad fue cortada». ‖ *cut* es el presente, pasado y participio pasado del verbo «cortar».

240

At a hotel.
A tired tourist asks the receptionist for a quiet room. When he's given the key, he asks:
—«Is this really a quiet hotel? I'm very tired and I need a rest.»
—«Yes, sir, of course, it is», replies the receptionist. «What's noisy are the people in it.»

when he's given the key, cuando le dan la llave. Literalmente: «cuando le es dada la llave». Esta es una forma muy corriente que se emplea con el verbo *give.* ‖ *given* es el participio pasado del verbo *give* (dar).

241

FIRST ENGLISH TEACHER: «There's a word in English which is always pronounced wrong by Spanish students.»
SECOND ENGLISH TEACHER: «Oh, yes, I know. You mean the word "wrong".»

which is always pronounced wrong by Spanish students, que siempre pronuncian mal los estudiantes españoles. Literalmente: «que siempre es pronunciada mal por (los) estudiantes españoles».

242

At an oral examination.
TEACHER: «What is wood used for?»
PUPIL (after thinking for a moment): «For making trees.»

what is wood used for?, ¿para qué se usa la madera? Esta es la forma corriente que se utiliza con preguntas que comienzan con palabra interrogativa *(what)* precedida de preposición *(for).* Nótese que la preposición pasa al final de la pregunta. La pregunta, desde un punto de vista estrictamente gramatical, sería: *for what is wood used for?*

243

OCULIST: «Have your eyes ever been checked before?»
PATIENT: «No, they've always been plain blue.»

have your eyes ever been checked before? ¿le han examinado los ojos alguna vez antes? Literalmente: «¿han sido sus ojos alguna vez comprobados antes?».
 || *checked* también significa «a cuadros», de ahí el chiste.
plain blue, azul liso.

244

At the police station.
DRUNK (indignantly): «I want to know why I've been arrested!»
POLICEMAN: «You've been brought here for drinking.»
DRUNK: «Ah, that's different! When are we going to start?»

you've been brought here for drinking, le han traído aquí por beber. También puede significar «para beber», de ahí el chiste. || Literalmente: «usted ha sido traído aquí...». || *brought* es el pasado y participio pasado de bring (traer).

245

Nick and David are watching their neighbour Joe Brown driving by in a new car.
NICK: «I can't understand how Joe can buy a new car when he hasn't even got enough money to catch the bus.»
DAVID: «Quite easy. Bus tickets can't be paid for in instalments.»

bus tickets can't be paid for in instalments, los billetes de autobús no pueden comprarse a plazos. Literalmente: «no pueden ser comprados a plazos». ‖ *to pay for something,* pagar algo. ‖ *paid* es el pasado y participio pasado de *pay* (pagar).

246

WILLY (to teacher): «Mr Baxter, can someone be punished for something he hasn't done?»
MR BAXTER: «Oh, no, Willy; of course not. Why do you ask?»
WILLY: «Because I haven't done my homework today.»

can someone be punished...? ¿le pueden castigar a alguien...? Literalmente: «¿puede alguien ser castigado...?».
done es el participio pasado de *do* (hacer).

247

Mr Hill was summoned for breaking the Highway Code. The moment the judge appeared in the room, Mr Hill, who hoped the judge would let him off, tried to appear very polite and said:
—«Good afternoon, sir. How are you? to which the judge said sternly: "Fine!".»

Mr Hill was summoned for breaking the Highway Code, a Mr Hill le mandaron una citación (fue citado) por trasgredir el Código de la Circulación.
who hoped the judge would let him off, que esperaba que el juez le absolviera.
fine, significa «bien», como respuesta a la pregunta: *How are you?*, y también «multa», de ahí el chiste.

248

MR NEIL: «Can I have tomorrow off to go and see my mother-in-law with my wife?»
BOSS: «I'm sorry, but you must come in tomorrow. There's a lot of work to be done at the office.»
MR NEIL: «Oh!, thank you, Mr Harris, I knew I could depend on you.»

can I have tomorrow off? ¿puedo tomarme el día libre mañana?
there's a lot to be done at the office, hay mucho que hacer en la oficina. Literalmente: «hay mucho (trabajo) que ser hecho». || *done* es el participio pasado de *do* (hacer).

249

Jack and Tom are talking about parapsychology.
JACK: «I've been following a course in parapsychology lately and now I am what could be called a thought-reader.»
TOM: «What's that?»
JACK: «I can read people's minds. For example I can tell you what you're thinking about at this very moment.»
TOM: «Oh, can you? Then, I beg your pardon.»

what could be called, lo que podría llamarse. Literalmente: «lo que podría ser llamado».
a thought-reader, una persona que lee el pensamiento.
at this very moment, en este mismo momento.

250

A millionaire is talking to his daughter's prospective husband.
—«I suppose that when you thought of marrying my daughter you were thinking of my money.»
—«Oh, no, sir. I'm not interested in your money. I want to marry your daughter because I love her.»
—«In that case, there's no more to be said. I don't want any fools in my family.»

I'm not interested in your money, no me interesa su dinero. Literalmente: «no estoy interesado en su dinero».

there's no more to be said, no hay más que decir. Literalmente: «no hay más (que) ser dicho». ‖ *said* es el pasado y participio pasado de *say* (decir).

EJERCICIOS

I. *Tradúzcase al inglés:*

1. ¿Es usted amigo del novio?
2. Betsy se casa mañana.
3. El guardia dijo: «¿Por qué va usted tan deprisa?» (conduciendo).
4. ¿Te apañas bien con el salario de tu marido?
5. Pareces un poco perplejo.
6. Doctor, quiero darle las gracias por su tratamiento.
7. ¿Por qué no contestas al teléfono?
8. ¿Está usted alguna vez en desacuerdo con su mujer?
9. Quiero asegurar todos los muebles de esta oficina menos el reloj.
10. No me interesa el trabajo.
11. Deme un billete de ida y vuelta a Windsor.
12. Hablemos cara a cara.
13. Eso no es totalmente verdad.
14. ¿Qué buscas? Busco un billete de cinco libras.
15. El tren llegó puntualmente.
16. ¿Fuiste a ver al médico a consultarle sobre tu pérdida de memoria?
17. Me dijo que le pagara por anticipado.
18. ¿Cómo es que tienes ese ojo negro?
19. ¿Cómo ocurrió?
20. ¿Dormiste bien anoche?

II. *Colóquense las preposiciones apropiadas en los espacios en blanco:*

1. My brother lost his watch .... the underground.
2. A man rang Mr Johnson's door-bell .... four o'clock .... the morning.

3. Mr Johnson got up .... bed and opened the door.
4. A tourist .... a motor-bike is going .... full speed .... the road .... Stratford-upon-Avon.
5. I don't want to go .... this bus.
6. He said that he was sick .... me.
7. My husband gave me this mink coat .... my birthday.
8. Have you anything .... grey hair?
9. A tourist arrives .... a village when the church bells are ringing.
10. There was a tap .... the door.
11. Do you manage all right .... your husband's salary?
12. Does this tree belong .... the coniferous family?
13. Do you ever disagree .... your wife?
14. I don't allow noisy people .... this house.
15. My son is .... the perfect age now.
16. To begin ...., let me tell you that I lead a very happy life.
17. I have a cottage .... the seaside.
18. Are you interested .... the job?
19. Give me a return ticket .... Windsor, please.
20. Don't trouble to see me .... the door, Mr Jones.

III. *Añádanse las partículas apropiadas a estos verbos compuestos:*

1. I see you've taken .... a new person to do the washing ....
2. She's just broken .... her engagement to Doctor Harris.
3. That electric fire has been .... all evening and it isn't very cold today.
4. I can't go .... with you. I'm married.
5. I've got to go shopping now. I'll be .... at about five.
6. How long will this go .... for?
7. When she grows .... she'll help us.
8. A motorist has just run .... a cat.
9. Can I have tomorrow .... to go and see my mother-in-law?
10. I can't cure you because you have nothing to give ....
11. We're .... of roses now, but we've got some very nice carnations.
12. I must get .... early to catch a train.
13. If you don't pay, I'll kick you .... of the restaurant.

14. How much do you charge for taking a tooth ....?
15. He took his watch .... to wind it ....
16. I don't know what Larry spends his money ....
17. What is green and goes round and round? I don't know. I give ....
18. My husband came .... of prison last Monday.
19. I'm looking .... a five-pound note.
20. The man got .... from bed and opened the door.

IV. *Después de haber leído los chistes de este libro, complétense los espacios en blanco con las palabras apropiadas:*

1. Girls are more beautiful than ....
2. We're out of ammunition. Then cease ....
3. Let's speak face to ....
4. Did your wife give you a hiding when you went .... late last Monday?
5. The train arrived at the .... on time.
6. Did you go to see the .... about your loss of memory?
7. Please put a .... on this envelope.
8. The teacher wrote a tactful .... to the boy's mother.
9. I send my boy to school for you to .... him.
10. How did you get that .... eye?
11. What on .... do you want at this time?
12. A tourist on a motor-bike is going at full .... along the road.
13. A drunk got on a double-decker ....
14. My husband gave me this mink coat for my 30th ....
15. Did you hear about old Tom? No, what happened to ....?
16. When I first .... a cigarette I got terrible pains in my stomach.
17. I want to insure all the furniture in this office .... the clock.
18. Do you manage all right on your husband's ....?
19. She has so many gold teeth that she sleeps with her head inside a ....
20. My brakes are out of order and I want to get home as soon as possible to avoid an ....

V. *Pónganse los artículos* the *o* a/an *donde sea necesario:*

1. .... girls are more beautiful than .... boys.
2. I'm .... bride's mother.
3. My uncle Ted had .... wooden leg.
4. I'm hurrying home to avoid .... accident.
5. Have you any difficulty with .... first question?
6. Why don't you like .... grapes?
7. You aren't .... patient of mine, are you?
8. Why don't .... elephants do .... military service?
9. .... carrots are very good for .... eyesight.
10. My daughter is at .... perfect age now.
11. Give me .... return ticket to Windsor, please.
12. Cease .... fire!
13. One day Mr and Mrs Roberts went to .... zoo.
14. Did you hear about .... old Tom?
15. Why did you have to leave .... school?
16. Today you say you don't like .... mushrooms!
17. I've asked for .... whisky .... hundred times.
18. At .... moment I'm selling cars.
19. .... finger-prints on .... plates are different now.
20. You'll find your lunch on .... page 45 of .... cookery book.

VI. *En el texto aparecen los siguientes verbos irregulares. Complétense con las dos formas que faltan:*

1. eat ....
2. get ....
3. drive ....
4. sleep ....
5. leave ....
6. teach ....
7. cost ....
8. think ....
9. put ....
10. do ....
11. wear ....
12. take ....
13. run ....

14. see ....
15. speak ....
16. go ....
17. mean ....
18. dream ....
19. smell ....
20. come ....

VII. *Tradúzcase al inglés:*

1. Un turista llega a un pueblo cuando las campanas de la iglesia están tocando y pregunta a un lugareño:
   «¿Por qué tocan hoy las campanas?»
   «Porque el cura está tirando de las cuerdas», responde el lugareño.

2. «Cuesta dos libras hablar con alguien en Birmingham.»
   «¿No hay una tarifa más barata para escuchar solamente? Quiero llamar a mi mujer.»

3. «¿Es usted amiga del novio?»
   «No, no lo soy. Soy la madre de la novia.»

VIII. *Colóquese el adjetivo apropiado acompañando a los sustantivos. Elíjanse de entre los siguientes:*

HOT - LONG - GREY - NOISY - BLACK - BLUE - FUNNY - TERRIBLE
BIG - WOODEN - STRANGE - PLEASED - THIN - DISGUSTING - QUIET
WONDERFUL - NEW - HUNGRY - WORRIED - SHABBY

1. My uncle Ted had a .... leg.
2. This chop has a .... taste.
3. I want to thank for your .... treatment, doctor.
4. I'm very .... to give this award to our hero.
5. .... sense of humour the plumber's got!
6. Have you anything for .... hair?
7. I see you've taken on a .... person to do the washing up.
8. Your husband must remain .... for a fortnight at least.

9. That's a very .... suit you're wearing, Murray.
10. If the baby turns .... the water is too cold.
11. If the baby turns red the water is too ....
12. I'm so .... that I can't sleep at all.
13. It would have been more .... to find half a worm inside the apple.
14. You used to be fat and now you're ....
15. Would you give me something to eat? I'm very ....
16. I don't allow .... people in this house.
17. You've been fighting those .... boys again!
18. I made a .... mistake.
19. How did you get that .... eye?
20. The waiter took a .... time to come between courses.

IX. *Colóquese el adverbio apropiado. Elíjase de entre los siguientes:*
BADLY - STERNLY - YET - AGO - EASILY - EARLY - NEVER YESTERDAY - FAST - ALREADY - ALWAYS - WELL - QUICKLY - EXACTLY - LATE.

1. Why are you driving so ....?
2. Does your roof .... leak? No, only when it rains.
3. The sign was stolen a month ....
4. That's what I call earning money ....
5. Yesterday I met a boy .... like you.
6. Are you the gentleman who wanted to get up .... to catch the seven o'clock train?
7. The sheriff looks .... at Bill, who has broken the law.
8. Mother taught me how to cook ....
9. Don't go to sleep ....
10. A tenant was playing the trumpet very .... at night.
11. I don't know how many cakes I've eaten ....
12. Mink wears ....
13. A school-boy was so dirty and smelled so .... that the teacher wrote a tactful letter to his mother.
14. Rabbits .... wear glasses.
15. This chop has a strange taste, so I'm eating it .... just to get rid of it.

X. *Palabras terminadas en -ing. Colóquese cada una en el lugar apropiado:*

BRUSHING - WEDDING - HESITATING - SLEEPING - DISGUSTING
HIDING - CORRECTING - SELLING - TELLING - PUTTING - YAWNING
LOOKING - GOING - FISHING - DRINKING - TALKING - CHARRING
FIGHTING - LIVING - SMELLING.

1. I'm .... in the water.
2. You've been .... those big boys again!
3. .... whisky is very bad for the health.
4. How can you keep sardines from ....?
5. Are you .... your teeth with my tooth-brush?
6. The photo you took of my .... group is horrible.
7. Bill, without .... exclaimed: «I'll take the hundred dollars!»
8. Here are some .... pills.
9. How ....! I've found a worm in this apple!
10. I'm .... to count my money before you give me the anaesthetic.
11. Go to sleep or I'll give you a ....
12. The teacher is .... the exercises.
13. I hear your wife has to support you by going out ....
14. Why aren't you .... any saucers under the cups?
15. What are you .... for?
16. Please stop .... and let me go to sleep.
17. He kept on .... while I was talking.
18. I don't like .... in this house.
19. My wife is always .... me she's going to leave me.
20. At the moment I'm .... cars.

SOLUCIONES

I.

1. Are you a friend of the bridegroom's?
2. Betsy is getting married tomorrow.
3. The policeman said to him: Why are you driving so fast?
4. Do you manage all right on your husband's salary?
5. You look a bit puzzled.
6. Doctor, I want to thank you for your treatment.
7. Why don't you answer the phone?
8. Do you ever disagree with your wife?
9. I want to insure all the furniture in this office except the clock.
10. I'm not interested in the job.
11. Give me a return ticket to Windsor.
12. Let's speak face to face.
13. That's not quite true.
14. What are you looking for? I'm looking for a five-pound note.
15. The train arrived on time.
16. Did you go to see the doctor about your loss of memory?
17. He told me to pay him in advance.
18. How did you get that black eye?
19. How did that happen?
20. Did you sleep well last night?

II.

1. in
2. at - in
3. from
4. on - at - along - to
5. on
6. of
7. for
8. for
9. at
10. on

11.	on	16.	with
12.	to	17.	at
13.	with	18.	in
14.	in	19.	to
15.	at	20.	to

III.

1.	on - up	11.	out
2.	off	12.	up
3.	on	13.	out
4.	out	14.	out
5.	back	15.	off - up
6.	on	16.	on
7.	up	17.	up
8.	over	18.	out
9.	off	19.	for
10.	up	20.	up

IV. *Los números entre paréntesis indican los chistes en que aparecen.*

1.	boys (1)	11.	earth (60)
2.	fire (38)	12.	speed (62)
3.	face (37)	13.	bus (64)
4.	home (41)	14.	birthday (69)
5.	station (43)	15.	him (52)
6.	doctor (49)	16.	smoked (53)
7.	stamp (54)	17.	except (29)
8.	letter (55)	18.	salary (13)
9.	teach (55)	19.	safe (11)
10.	black (59)	20.	accident (10)

V.

1.	(-) (-)	4.	an
2.	the	5.	the
3.	a	6.	(-)

GRAMMAR AND HUMOUR

7. a
8. (-) (-)
9. (-) - the
10. the
11. a
12. (-)
13. the
14. (-)
15. (-)
16. (-)
17. a - a
18. the
19. the - the
20. (-) - the

VI.

1. ate, eaten
2. got, got
3. drove, driven
4. slept, slept
5. left, left
6. taught, taught
7. cost, cost
8. thought, thought
9. put, put
10. did, done
11. wore, worn
12. took, taken
13. ran, run
14. saw, seen
15. spoke, spoken
16. went, gone
17. meant, meant
18. dreamt, dreamt
19. smelt, smelt
20. came, come

VII. Solución del 1.º, chiste núm. 6.
Solución del 2.º, chiste núm. 18.
Solución del 3.º, chiste núm. 2.

VIII.

1. wooden
2. strange
3. wonderful
4. pleased
5. funny
6. grey
7. new
8. quiet
9. shabby
10. blue
11. hot
12. worried
13. disgusting
14. thin
15. hungry
16. noisy
17. big
18. terrible
19. black
20. long

IX.

1. fast
2. always
3. ago
4. easily
5. exactly
6. early
7. sternly
8. yesterday
9. yet
10. late
11. already
12. well
13. badly
14. never
15. quickly

X.

1. fishing
2. fighting
3. drinking
4. smelling
5. brushing
6. wedding
7. hesitating
8. sleeping
9. disgusting
10. going
11. hiding
12. correcting
13. charring
14. putting
15. looking
16. talking
17. yawning
18. living
19. telling
20. selling

PUNTOS LINGÜISTICOS

Relación de algunos puntos lingüísticos de interés que aparecen en los textos. (Las cifras corresponden a la numeración de los chistes. Sólo se señala un ejemplo en cada caso.)

About = acerca de, 91
About = aproximadamente, 136
About to = a punto de, 135
Acusativo + infinitivo, 49
Adjetivos (grado comparativo, más de una sílaba), 1
Adjetivos (grado comparativo, una sílaba), 18
Adjetivos (grado superlativo, una sílaba), 27
Adverbios (comparación), 109
Adverbios terminados en «*ly*», 1
After como preposición, 104
All entre sujeto y verbo, 81
All entre verbo auxiliar y principal, 88
Already, 122
Already entre verbo auxiliar y principal, 88
Always después del verbo *to be*, 105
Always entre sujeto y verbo, 14
Another como adjetivo, 122
Another como pronombre, 70
Artículo determinado (omisión), 25, 66
As = como (a título de), 91
As = cuando, 193
As = ya que, 174
Before como conjunción. Ej.: *before you give me...*, 114
Before como preposición. Ej.: *before his operation...*, 114
Between = entre (dos términos), 89
Between seguido de plural, con la idea de «entre uno y otro», 47
Bring combinado con dos objetos (directo/indirecto), 109
By + agente, 241
By = al lado de, 229

By + gerundio (indicando medio, método), 215
By = por medio de, 239
Each, 81
Each other (pronombre recíproco), 200
Either... or, 176
Either = tampoco, 71
Estaciones del año, 228
Ever, 24, 105
Every, 87
For = durante, 219
For = por, 223
For + gerundio = para + infinitivo, 227
For + gerundio = por/para + infinitivo, 224
For + gerundio = por + infinitivo, 76
Genitivo sajón *(Double Genitive)*. Ej.: *are you a friend of the bridegroom's?*, 2
Genitivo sajón *(Inflected Genitive)*. Ej.: *the bride's mother*, 2
Genitivo sajón *(Local Genitive)*. Ej.: *at the chemist's*, 5
Get + adjetivo, 111
Get to + lugar, 48
Give con dos objetos (directo/indirecto), 65
Hand con dos objetos (directo/indirecto), 35
Have = tomar, 209
Have + *got* = tener, 103
Have to, 66
Hear = oír, 220
Hear = tener entendido, 203
How después del verbo *learn*, 113
How después del verbo *teach*, 180
How en exclamaciones, 53
How en preguntas, 90
How en frase interrogativa indirecta, 185
How many?, 209
How much?, 210
Infinitivo *(Anaphoric to)*. Ej.: *refused to*, 63
Infinitivo después de adjetivo. Ej.: *you're very hard to please*, 72
Infinitivo después de sustantivo. Ej.: *money to buy them*, 85
Infinitivo sin *to (Plain Infinitive)*. Ej.: *to help a lady change a wheel*, 225
Infinitivo sin *to (Plain Infinitive)*. Ej.: *don't let her go!*, 63
Infinitivo sin *to* precedido de *why (Plain Infinitive)*, 165

Instead of + gerundio, 216
Instead of + sustantivo, 80
Just + participio pasado = acabar de, 124
Just = solamente, únicamente, 42
Like = como, 198
Like + gerundio, 220
Look + adjetivo, 69
Look como sustantivo, 144
Look like + sustantivo, 237
Look (at) = mirar, 237
Never entre sujeto y verbo, 26
Never entre verbo auxiliar y principal, 89
No como adverbio de negación, 2
No + sustantivo = ningún, 71
Nor = tampoco
One = cierto. Ej.: *one day*, 70
One como pronombre. Ej.: *a blue one*, 70
One como pronombre, seguido de *of*, 50
One precedido de *that*, 131
One = uno solo. Ej.: *one husband*, 70
Only entre verbo auxiliar y principal, 79
Only entre verbo defectivo y verbo principal, 137
Only = único, 183
Or, 30
Other como adjetivo, 216
Presente continuo combinado con *always* para indicar algo no deseable que se repite, 105
Question tags (¿Verdad?), 20
Sell con dos objetos (directo/indirecto), 110
Send con dos objetos (directo/indirecto), 143
So + adjetivo = tan + adjetivo, 93
So + adjetivo + *that* = tan + adjetivo + que, 89
So + adverbio = tan + adverbio, 62
So en puesto de una oración, 231
So = por tanto, 12
So = también. Ej.: *so have most people*, 175
Tell con dos objetos (directo/indirecto), 8
Till, 46
That como adjetivo demostrativo, 44
That como conjunción (después de verbo), 66
That como pronombre demostrativo, 80

That (conjunción omitida después de verbo). Ej.: *why do you say (that) this man was drunk?*, 95
This como adjetivo demostrativo, 14
This como pronombre demostrativo, 43
Too + adjetivo, 31
Too = también, 139
Trouble como verbo y sustantivo, 36
What en exclamaciones, 52
What en preguntas, 7
What = lo que, 116
Who en preguntas, 16
Who introduciendo oración sustantiva objeto directo, 117
Who como pronombre relativo, 176, 179
Why...? Because..., 6
Yet al final de oración, 127
Yet precedido de *not*, 74

FRASES HECHAS

Frases hechas que aparecen en los textos. (Las cifras hacen referencia a la numeración de los chistes.)

Be careful, 225
Can I have a word with you?, 156
Don't wait for me, 178
Don't worry, 101
Don't you remember me?, 173
Go to sleep, 109
How are you?, 247
How did that happen?, 56
How do you fell today?, 73
How long will this go on for?, 111
How much do you charge for...?, 213
How's that?, 50
I beg your pardon, 249
I don't know, 7
I haven't got enough money, 163
I think it's too late now, 237
I want to buy a..., 112
I wish you good luck, 65
I'd like a..., 128
I'll be back at about five, 107
I'm not interested in..., 250
I'm so glad, 130
I'm sorry, 248
I'm sorry, but I can't, 166
I'm very hungry, 146
I'm very sorry, 142
I'm very tired and I need a rest, 240
In that case, 250
Is that Mr Jackson?, 185
It's only a question of five minutes, 213

It's quite common, 175
It's too far away, 236
It's very easy, 205
Just now, 172
Let me think, 233
Listen, 132
Look here, 160
Never mind, 166
Of course, 168
Thank goodness, 192
Thank you, 14
That's different, 244
That's not too bad, 201
That's true, 144
There's a lot of work to be done, 248
There's no more to be said, 250
To begin with, 32
Wait a moment, 146
Well done!, 43
What are you looking for?, 40
What bad luck!, 52
What does... mean?, 42
What was wrong?, 66
What would you do in my place?, 204
What's that?, 249
What's the matter?, 163
What's the matter with you?, 171
What's your full name?, 147
What's your problem?, 32
Where does he live?, 110
Why do you ask?, 182
Why not?, 17
Why was that?, 53
Would you give me something to eat?, 146
You needn't worry, 175
You've been very kind to me, 223

VOCABULARIO

Este vocabulario no incluye todas las palabras del texto sino sólo aquéllas que pueden presentar dificultad. (La traducción al español de los adjetivos aparece en su forma de masculino solamente.)

according to, de acuerdo con.
afford, permitirse el lujo.
airhostess, azafata.
air-liner, avión de línea.
aloud, en voz alta.
anaesthetic, anestesia.
angler, pescador (de caña).
angry, enfadado.
announcer, locutor.
anyhow, de todos modos.
apologize, pedir perdón.

appear, aparecer.
argue, discutir.
as, como, ya que.
assure, asegurar.
astonished, asombrado.
asylum, manicomio.
attendant, acomodador.
aunt, tía.
avoid, evitar.
award, premio.
awful, terrible.

back, parte de atrás.
baker, panadero.
bald, calvo.
bandaged, vendado.
basement, sótano.
bath, bañar.
beam, viga.
beard, barba.
beating, paliza.
believe, crecer.
belong, pertenecer.
bell, campana, timbre.
bill, pico (de ave), cuenta (factura).

boring, aburrido.
borrow, pedir prestado.
boss, jefe.
bowl, plato hondo.
boyfriend, novio.
brake, freno.
bricklayer, albañil.
bride, novia.
bridegroom, novio.
brush, cepillar, cepillo.
bump, chichón.
burst, reventar.
butcher, carnicero.

bite, morder.
blouse, blusa.
bomber, bombardero.

cabinet, vitrina.
capsule, cápsula.
carnation, clavel.
carriage, vagón.
carrot, zanahoria.
case, caso.
catch, tomar (el autobús, tren, etc.).
chance, oportunidad.
change, cambiar, cambio.
charge, cobrar.
chauffeur, chófer.
check, comprobar.
cheek, cara dura.
chicken, pollo.
choose, elegir.
chop, chuleta.
clean, limpio.
clerk, empleado.

dangerous, peligroso.
darling, querido, a.
debt, deuda.
deck, piso (de un autobús).
degree, título.
deliver, entregar.
depend, depender.
design, diseño, dibujo.
diet, dieta.
dig, cavar.
disagree, no estar de acuerdo.
disappointed, decepcionado.
discover, descubrir.

button, botón.
buy, comprar.

climb up, trepar.
coat, chaqueta, abrigo.
coin, moneda.
Commandments, Mandamientos.
complain, quejarse.
conductor, cobrador (de un vehículo).
cook, cocinero, cocinar.
corner, esquina, rincón.
corridor, pasillo.
cottage, chalet.
course, curso, plato (de un menú).
cousin, primo.
cross, cruzar.
cupboard, armario.
cure, curar, cura.
curious, curioso.
customer, cliente.

disease, enfermedad.
disgusting, asqueroso.
dismiss, despedir.
dissolve, disolverse.
doorbell, timbre (de la puerta).
dowry, dote.
dozen, docena.
drive by, pasar en coche.
driver, conductor.
drop in, entrar al pasar.
drunk, borracho.
dust, polvo.
dust-bin, cubo de basura.

earn, ganar (sueldo).
either, tampoco (con neg.).
elderly, entrado en años.
embarrassed, azorado.
empty, vacío.
enclosure, recinto.
engage, contratar.
engagement, compromiso.
engine-driver, maquinista.

engraved, grabado.
enough, bastante.
envelope, sobre.
essay, redacción.
eventually, finalmente.
ever, alguna vez.
examinee, examinando.
expect, esperar.
eyesight, vista.

factory, fábrica.
fair, justo, rubio.
false, falso.
farm, granja, finca.
fat, grueso.
fees, honorarios.
fetch, ir a buscar, ir por.
fiancée, novia.
finger-print, huella digital.
fish, pescar.
fishmonger, pescadero.
fiver, billete de cinco libras.
flat, piso.

flirt, flirtear.
follow, seguir.
fool, tonto.
forehead, frente.
forget, olvidar.
form, formulario.
fortnight, quincena.
free, gratis.
fridge, frigorífico.
frog, rana.
funny, gracioso.
fur, piel (de abrigo).
furniture, mobiliario.

gamekeeper, guardabosque.
gargle, hacer gárgaras.
give up, dejar (abandonar).
gloomy, tétrico.
gossip, cotilla.
grandson, nieto.

granny, abuelita.
grapes, uvas.
great-great-grandfather, tatarabuelo.
grocer, tendero.
guess, adivinar.

hammer, martillo.
hand, mano, entregar.
happen, ocurrir.
harm, daño.
harmful, dañino, perjudicial.
health, salud.

healthy, sano.
height, altura.
heir, heredero.
help, ayudar.
helper, ayudante.
hesitate, vacilar.

hiding, paliza.
hole, agujero.
homework, tarea escolar.
hose, manguera.
housewife, ama de casa.

hum, tatarear.
hungry, hambriento.
husband, marido.
hurry, apresurarse.

illness, enfermedad.
insomnia, insomnio.
instalments, plazos.
insure, asegurar.

interviewer, entrevistador.
invigilator, vigilante (en un examen).
iron, hierro, plancha, planchar.

jack, gato (para levantar un coche).
jail, cárcel.
jaundice, ictericida.

jeweller, joyero.
jump, salto.

kick, dar una patada, patada.
kill, matar.
kind, amable.
kiss, besar, beso.

kitchen, cocina.
knife, cuchillo.
knock, golpe, llamar (a la puerta).

land, aterrizar, ir a parar, tierra.
landlady, patrona.
lately, últimamente.
lavatory, lavabo (habitación).
law, ley.
laziness, vagancia.
lazy, vago.
leak, gotear.
leave, dejar.
lend, prestar.

light, luz.
lightning, rayo.
lips, labios.
live, vivir.
locked, cerrado con llave.
lose, perder.
loss, pérdida.
luck, suerte.
lucky, afortunado.
lump, terrón.

mahogany, caoba.
major, comandante.
make up, maquillaje.
manicurist, manicura.
married, casado.

mate, compañero.
meet, encontrarse.
mention, mencionar.
mind, mente.
mine-field, campo de minas.

mink, visón.
mistake, equivocación.
moon, luna.
motor-bike, moto.

motorist, automovilista.
moustache, bigote.
move, mudarse (de casa).
mushrooms, champiñones.

naughty, travieso.
neck, cuello.
need, necesitar.
neighbour, vecino.
neighbourhood, vecindad.
New Zealand, Nueva Zelanda.

newspaper, periódico.
noisy, ruidoso.
noodles, fideos.
note, billete.
notice, notar.
nursing home, sanatorio.

officer, oficial.
omelette, tortilla.
once, una vez.
onion, cebolla.
orphan, huérfano.

overheard, oído por casualidad.
owe, deber (algo).
own, propio.
owner, dueño, propietario.
oyster, ostra.

pain, dolor.
paper, papel, periódico.
parapsychology, parapsicología.
paratrooper, paracaidista.
parcel, paquete.
parrot, loro.
path, camino, vereda, senda.
patient, paciente.
pay, pagar.
pay back, devolver (lo que se debe).
payday, día de cobro.
peace, paz.
pearl, perla.
pet, animal de compañía.
pick, coger (fruta).
pickpocket, ratero.
pinch, pellizcar.
pill, píldora.

play, obra de teatro.
pleased, contento.
pleasure, placer.
plumber, fontanero.
pocket, bolsillo.
pole, poste.
polish, lustrar.
polite, cortés.
porter, portero.
positive, seguro.
post, correo.
present, regalo.
press, apretar.
priest, cura.
prize, premio.
proof, prueba.
prospective, en perspectiva.
protest, protestar.
psychiatrist, psiquiatra.

pull, tirar de.
punish, castigar.

push, empujar, empujón.
puzzled, perplejo.

quiet, tranquilo.

rabbit, conejo.
rate, tarifa.
razor, maquinilla de afeitar.
realize, darse cuenta.
reason, razón.
receipt, recibo.
receiver, auricular (del teléfono).
recognize, reconocer.
recruit, recluta.
refuse, negarse.
rent, alquilar.
replace, reemplazar.
rescue, rescate, rescatar.
respect, respeto.
rest, descansar, descanso.

return, volver.
reward, recompensa.
rich, rico.
ride, paseo en coche.
rise, aumento de sueldo.
ring, sortija, sonar, tocar (campana, timbre).
road, carretera.
robbery, robo.
roof, tejado.
rope, cuerda.
rose, rosa.
ruler, regla.
run over, atropellar.

safe, caja de caudales.
salary, sueldo.
saucer, platillo.
save, ahorrar.
scarf, pañuelo de cuello, bufanda.
seaside, costa.
seat, asiento.
sell, vender.
send, enviar.
sew, coser.
shabby, raído.
shave, afeitarse.
shirt, camisa.
shop, tienda.
shop-assistant, dependiente.
shout, gritar.
shower, ducha.

sideboard, aparador.
sign, señal, cartel.
silver, plata.
sleep, dormir.
slippery, resbaladizo.
slot, ranura.
smart, elegante.
smell, olor, oler.
snag, pega.
sob, sollozar.
soup, sopa.
spend, gastar.
stable, establo.
stagger out, salir dando tumbos.
stamp, sello (de correos).
start, poner en marcha.
statistics, estadística.

steal, robar.
sternly, con cara de pocos amigos, de malos modos.
stomach, estómago.
stone, peso de 14 libras.
successfully, con éxito.
suddenly, de repente.
suit, sentar bien, traje.
summon, citar.

tactful, discreto.
talk, charla, hablar.
taste, gusto, catar.
tear, lágrima.
teeth, dientes, muelas.
tenant, inquilino.
thief, ladrón.
thin, delgado.
tie, corbata.
time, tiempo, vez.
tin, lata.
tip, propina.
tongs, tenazas.

uncle, tío.
underground, metro (medio de locomoción).
undertaker, empresario de pompas fúnebres.

vacuum cleaner, aspiradora.
villager, lugareño.

wallet, cartera.
wash-basin, lavabo (mueble).
wasteful, derrochador.
watch, mirar, quedarse, mirando, reloj.

supper, cena.
support, mantener.
sure, seguro.
surprise, sorpresa.
suspicious, sospechoso.
swallow, tragar.
swear, decir palabrotas.
sweet, caramelo, dulce.

tongue, lengua.
tooth, diente, muela.
tooth-brush, cepillo de dientes.
towards, hacia.
tray, bandeja.
treat, tratar.
trigger, gatillo.
trip, tropezar.
trouble, molestia, molestar.
trout, trucha, truchas.
truthful, veraz.
twice, dos veces.

use, usar, uso.
useful, útil.

VIP, Very Important Person.
voice, voz.

water, agua, regar.
wedding, boda.
wheel, rueda.
whistle, silbato, silbido.
whole, completo.

wife, esposa.
wind up, dar cuerda.
wine, vino.
wish, desear, deseo.
without, sin.
wood, madera.
wooden, de madera.

word, palabra.
worm, gusano.
worried, preocupado.
worry, preocuparse.
wrinkled, arrugado.
wrist, muñeca.
wrong, mal, equivocado.

yawn, bostezar.

yet, todavía.

From the same publisher

Libros didácticos complementarios - Resource Material

Grammar & Reference Books

El inglés compendiado. An Easy English Grammar. Manual muy completo, claro, práctico y esquemático de gramática inglesa.

Las dificultades idiomáticas del inglés. Resuelve de manera muy práctica las dificultades que se presentan con mayor frecuencia.

Sinónimos ingleses explicados. English Synonyms Explained. Cuando un estudiante de inglés busca en el diccionario una palabra, p.ej. "mirar" encuentra: *Glance, Stare, Contemplate, Gaze, Watch, etc.* ¿Cuál elegir? Este libro explica cada palabra desde un punto de vista práctico.

Practice in Translation Spanish-English.

Manual práctico de traducción inversa. Español-inglés. Contiene más de 1.000 ejercicios de traducción del español al inglés, desde la frase al texto. Con alternativas.

Textos literarios para traducir. Español-inglés. Nivel avanzado. Textos literarios de autores contemporáneos de habla española traducidos al inglés con numerosas notas y variantes alternativas. Muy útil para alumnos avanzados y opositores.

Specialized Dictionaries

Catálogo de expresiones para la traducción inversa. Español-inglés. Más de 7.000 expresiones de uso corriente que facilitan tanto la expresión oral como escrita.

Diccionario auxiliar del traductor. Español-inglés. The Translator's Auxiliary Dictionary. Más de 5.000 frases de uso corriente para ilustrar el uso de las palabras del lenguaje cotidiano.

English False Friends. Palabras inglesas engañosas. Selección de palabras inglesas cuyo parecido con otras españolas es motivo de equivocaciones. Con ejercicios y soluciones.

English Slang. Inglés - Español. Más de 2.000 expresiones de slang de inglés cotidiano.

Diccionario de dudas del inglés. Diccionario excepcional que analiza y resuelve las dudas del estudiante español.

English Pronunciation Books

La pronunciación inglesa. Fonética y fonología. A Handbook of English Pronunciation. (Con cassette). (9ª ed.) Estudio práctico de los sonidos ingleses. Ilustrado con 50 dibujos y 10 fotos. Nivel básico.

Ejercicios de transcripción fonética en inglés. Contiene 45 párrafos graduados para practicar la transcripción fonética inglesa. Desde la frase al texto. Con notas y soluciones.

Práctica de pronunciación inglesa. English Pronunciation Practice. Contiene 75 ejercicios de entrenamiento auditivo. Con soluciones y transcripción fonética de las palabras.

Miscellaneous English

Refranes ingleses para estudiantes de inglés. Selección de 500 refranes ingleses, con su traducción o equivalencia en español, interpretación, puntos lingüísticos, ideas afines y notas.

English in Flashes. Más de 300 puntos lingüísticos ingleses de uso corriente y de diversa dificultad, presentados de forma breve, clara y muy sencilla.

Juegos de palabras en inglés. Selección de "piruetas lingüísticas" basadas en el doble sentido de las palabras.

Catálogo Gratuito

Solicite gratuitamente nuestro catálogo completo y totalmente actualizado de *Libros Didácticos Complementarios* escribiendo a la siguiente dirección, o llamando al teléfono que se indica.

Anglo-Didáctica Publishing
C/ Santiago de Compostela, 16 – bajo B
28034 Madrid, España
Tel y Fax: (34) 91 378 01 88